BREAKING SILENCE,
AN ANTHOLOGY OF
CONTEMPORARY
ASIAN AMERICAN POETS

BREAKING SILENCE, AN ANTHOLOGY OF CONTEMPORARY ASIAN AMERICAN POETS

BREAKING SILENCE,
An Anthology of Contemporary
Asian American Poets

Edited by Joseph Bruchac
The Greenfield Review Press
Greenfield Center, N.Y. 12833

Publication of this book has been made possible, in part, through a grant from the Literature Program of the National Endowment for the Arts.

Acknowledgements appear on the following pages.

Library of Congress Cataloguing in Publication Data:
Bruchac, Joseph, 1942—comp. BREAKING SILENCE, An Anthology of Contemporary Asian American Poets
contents: Mei-mei Berssenbrugge.—Luis Cabalquinto.—
Virginia Cerenio. (etc.) 1. American Poetry—Asian American Authors. 2. American Poetry—20th century
Library of Congress Catalogue Card 83-80759

ISBN 0-912678-59-3

FIRST EDITION

Cover photograph by Jack Lynch

Acknowledgements

Some of the poems in this anthology have previously appeared in the following publications. In all cases, permission to reprint has been granted by the individual authors. The importance of the magazines and presses cited on the following pages cannot be stressed strongly enough. They play an important and continuing role in the support of contemporary Asian American poetry.

Mei-Mei Berssenbrugge: ROOF for "Farolita."

Luis Cabalquinto: THE GREENFIELD REVIEW for "The Big One," AMERICAN BORN AND FOREIGN (SUNBURY 7-8, 1979) for "Hometown," "Eating Lechon, With My Brothers & Sisters."

Virginia Cerenio: EAST WIND MAGAZINE, 1983 for "manong benny," WOMEN TALKING WOMEN LISTENING, Volume III, 1977 for "pinay."

Diana Chang: THE HORIZON IS DEFINITELY SPEAKING, Backstreet Editions, for all selections included, as well as original publication in THE VIRGINIA QUARTERLY REVIEW, THE NEW YORK QUARTERLY, and BRIDGE.

Fay Chiang: MIWA'S SONG, Sunbury Press, N.Y. 1983 for all selections.

Marilyn Chin: MASSACHUSETTS REVIEW for "We Are A Young Nation, Uncle," BROWN REVIEW for "A Chinaman's Chance."

Eric Chock: TEN THOUSAND WISHES, Bamboo Ridge Press, 1978 for "Papio," and "Pulling Weeds." BAMBOO RIDGE No. 4, September 1979 for "The Mango Tree" and "Termites."

Jessica Hagedorn: PET FOOD & TROPICAL APPARITIONS, Momo's Press, San Francisco, 1983 for all selections.

Kimiko Hahn: COLUMBIA: A MAGAZINE OF POETRY AND PROSE for "When You Leave" and "Dance Instructios for a Young Girl." THE AGNI REVIEW for "A Girl Combs Her Hair."

Diane Hai-Jew: MATRIX, University of Washington for all selections.

Gail N. Harada: BAMBOO RIDGE: THE HAWAII WRITERS' QUARTERLY, No. 13, December 1981 for "Painted Passages," HAWAII REVIEW 8, Fall 1978 for "New Year," TALK STORY: AN ANTHOLOGY OF HAWAII'S LOCAL WRITERS, 1978, Petronium Press & Talk Story, Inc. for "First Winter," and WAHINE O HAWAII, SEAWEEDS & CONSTRUCTIONS No. 4, December 1977, Elepaio Press for "Pomegranate."

Garrett Kaoru Hongo: THE GREENFIELD REVIEW for "Hiking Up Heizan..."

Patricia Y. Ikeda: FIELD, Number 27, Fall 1982, Oberlin College, Oberlin, Ohio for "A Card Game: Kinjiro Sawada."

Yuri Kageyama: BRIDGE, 1978-79 for "Love Poem" (originally published as "For All You Brothers Out There), OBRAS (Beyond Baroque) for "A Day in a Long Hot Summer," SOUP, 1981 for "Disco Chinatown," THE ASIAN JOURNAL, 1980 for "Strings/Himo," THE GREENFIELD REVIEW for "My Mother Takes a Bath."

Lonny Kaneko: AMERASIA JOURNAL, Summer, 1975 for "Family Album," THE GREENFIELD REVIEW for "Violets for Mother."

Joy Kogawa: A CHOICE OF DREAMS, McClelland and Stewart, Ltd., Toronto, 1974 for all selections.

Tina Koyama: THE ARTS for "Grape Daiquiri," INTRO 13 for "Next," POET & CRITIC for "Ojisan After the Stroke: Three Notes to Himself," WILLOW SPRINGS for "Definitions of the Word Gout."

Geraldine Kudaka: NUMEROUS AVALANCHES AT THE POINT OF INTERSECTION, Greenfield Review Press, 1979 for "Okinawa Kanashii Monogatari," "On Writing Asian American Poetry."

8704013

Alex Kuo: NEW LETTERS FROM HIROSHIMA, Greenfield Review Press, 1974 and SHENANDOAH, Volume XXIII, Number 1, Fall 1971 for "Loss," NEW LETTERS, Volume 38, Number 1, Fall 1971 for "On A Clear Day I Can See Forever," and ARTS IN SOCIETY, Volume IV, Number III, Fall-Winter, 1967 for "There is Something I Want to Say."

Alan Chong Lau: EAST/WEST, 1983 for "day of the parade," EAST WIND for "living in the world," HOMEGROWN for "father takes to the road," SONGS FOR JADINA, Greenfield Review Press, 1980 for "crossing portsmouth bridge."

Deborah Lee: FRAGMENTS for "Words from a Bottle" (originally published as "Reflecting Before a Bottle").

Genny Lim: THIS BRIDGE CALLED MY BACK, Persephone, 1981 for "Wonder Woman."

Stephen Shu Ning Liu: THE ANTIOCH REVIEW, Summer 1981 for "My Father's Martial Art" (Also published in THE PUSHCART PRIZE, VII, 1982), SHENAN-DOAH, Fall 1977 for "Adultery at a Las Vegas Bookstore," NORTHWEST REVIEW, Vol. XVIII, 1980 for "On Pali Lookout," and CONTEMPORARY QUARTERLY, No. 10, 1980 for "A Pair of Fireflies."

Wing Tek Lum: BAMBOO RIDGE, No. 13, December 1981 for "The Poet Imagines His Grandfather's Thoughts on the Day He Died," POETRY, Volume CXL, No. 2, May 1982 for "To the Old Masters," BAMBOO RIDGE, No. 9, December 1980 for "Chinatown Games," and MANA Volume 6, No. 1, 1981 for "Translations."

Laureen Mar: THE SEATTLE TIMES for "The Immigration Act of 1924," TURNING SHADOWS INTO LIGHT (Young Pine Press) for "At Wonder Donut," LIVING FURNITURE (Noro Press) for "The Window Frames the Moon."

Diane Mei Lin Mark: IMPULSE, Fall 1976 for "Liberation," THIRD WORLD WOMEN, San Francisco Community Press, 1972 and ASIAN AMERICANS IN HAWAII, U. of Hawaii, 1975 for "Kula . . . A Homecoming," PEARLS, Springfield, Va, Educational Film Center, 1979 for "Suzie Wong Doesn't Live Here," and "And the Old Folks Said."

Janice Mirikitani: AMERASIA JOURNAL, Vol. 8 #2 for "Breaking Silence."

David Mura: THE AMERICAN POETRY REVIEW, Vol. 11, No. 4, July/August 1982 for "Lan Nguyen: The Uniform of Death," and January/February 1981, Vol. 10, No. 1 for "The Natives," and ANOTHER CHICAGO MAGAZINE, No. 7, 1982 for "Relocation."

Dwight Okita: ANOTHER CHICAGO MAGAZINE for "Crossing with the Light," and BANYAN ANTHOLOGY for "The Art of Shopping."

Arthur Sze: READ STREET for "moenkopi," NEW LETTERS for "Dazzled," CON-TACT II for "Black Lightning," LA CONFLUENCIA for "The Cloud Chamber." All selections also appear in the book DAZZLED, Floating Island Publications, 1983.

Jeff Tagami: TRANSFER, 1981 for "Without Names" and TRANSFER, 1982 for "Stonehouse."

Kitty Tsui: THE WORDS OF A WOMAN WHO BREATHES FIRE, Spinsters Ink, 1983 for "it's in the name" and "chinatown talking story."

George Uba: POETRY/LA 4, Spring-Summer 1982 for "How Do You Spell Missile."

Cyn Zarco: CALAFIA: THE CALIFORNIA POETRY, I. Reed Books, 1978 for "lolo died yesterday" and ESSENCE Magazine, November 1982 for "Saxophonetyx"

CONTENTS

Mei-mei Berssenbrugge   1

Farolita

Luis Cabalquinto   4

Blue Tropic
The Flower Vendor
The Big One
Eating Lechon, With My Brothers & Sisters
Hometown

Virginia Cerenio   10

You lovely people
Pinay
pick-up at rizal restaurant
manong benny
we who carry the endless seasons . . .

Diana Chang   16

Artists East and West
The Horizon is Definitely Speaking
Once and Future
Codes
Second Nature

Fay Chiang   21

Snow
A Letter to Peter
Voices That Have Filled My Day

Marilyn Chin   27

Write, Do Write
Grandmother Poems
The Landlord's Wife
We are a Young Nation, Uncle
A Chinaman's Chance

Eric Chock   33

Papio
Pulling Weeds
The Mango Tree
Termites

Cyril Dabydeen   39

Folklore
Lives
Rehearsal
Posterity
Rhapsodies

Jessica Hagedorn   44

Motown/Smokey Robinson
The Woman Who Thought She Was More Than a Samba
Ming the Merciless
Song for my Father

Kimiko Hahn   53

When You Leave
Daughter
Dance Instructions for a Young Girl
A Girl Combs Her Hair

Dianne Hai-Jew   57

Days Ago
Thirst of the Dragon
This Night
Foreign Soil

Gail N. Harada   63

First Winter
New Year
Pomegranate
Painted Passages

Garret Kaoru Hongo   70

Hiking Up Hieizan with Alan Lau/Buddha's Birthday 1974

Patricia Y. Ikeda   77

A Card Game: Kinjiro Sawada
Recovery
Translations

Lawson Inada   83

Since When as Ever More

Jaime Jacinto   89

Reflections on the Death of a Parrot
The Fire Breather, Mexico City
The Beads
Looking for Buddha

Yuri Kageyama   95

Love Poem
A Day in a Long Hot Summer
Disco Chinatown
Strings/Himo
My Mother Takes A Bath

Lonny Kaneko   103

Coming Home From Camp
The Secret
Violets for Mother
Family Album

Joy Kogawa   111

Ancestors' Graves in Kurakawa
On Meeting the Clergy of the Holy Catholic Church in Osaka
Hiroshima Exit
Dream After Touring the Tokyo Tokei
Woodtick

Tina Koyama   116

Grape Daiquiri
Definitions of the Word *Gout*
Ojisan After the Stroke: Three Notes to Himself
Next

Geraldine Kudaka   120

Okinawa Kanashii Monogatari
On Writing Asian-American Poetry
Giving Up ButterFlies
Death is a Second Cousin Dining with Us Tonight
Birthright

Alex Kuo   128

Did You Not See
Loss
An Early Illinois Winter
On A Clear Day I Can See Forever
There is Something I Want to Say

Alan Chong Lau   134

crossing portsmouth bridge
letters from kazuko
father takes to the road and lets his hair down
day of the parade
living in the world

Deborah Lee   142

Where He Hangs His Hat
You're Sorry, Your Mother is Crazy, & I'm a Chinese Shiksa
WOMEN OPEN CAUTIOUSLY
Words From A Bottle
Taking Care Of It

George Leong   148

This is our music
a sometimes love poem

Walter Lew   151

Leaving Seoul: 1953
Urn I: Silent For Twenty-Five Years, The Father of My Mother Advises Me
Fan
Two Handfuls of *Waka* for Thelonious Sphere Monk (d. Feb. 1982)

Genny Lim   159

Visiting Father
Departure
Sweet 'n Sour
Wonder Woman

Stephen Shu Ning Liu   165

My Father's Martial Art
I Lie On The Chilled Stones of the Great Wall
Adultery at a Las Vegas Bookstore
On Pali Lookout
A Pair of Fireflies

Wing Tek Lum   171

The Poet Imagines His Grandfather's Thoughts on the Day He Died
Translations
Chinatown Games
To The Old Masters
At A Chinaman's Grave

Laureen Mar   178

Black Rocks
At Wonder Donut
The Immigration Act of 1924
The Window Frames The Moon

Diane Mei Lin Mark   183

Rice and Rose Bowl Blues
Liberation
And the Old Folks Said
Kula .. A Homecoming
Suzie Wong Doesn't Live Here

Janice Mirikitani   188

Breaking Silence
Breaking Tradition

Jim Mitsui   193

Shakuhachi
When Father Came Home For Lunch
Letter to Tina Koyama from Elliot Bay Park
Mexico City, 150 Pesos to the Dollar
Graffiti in a University Restroom

David Mura   199

The Hibakusha's Letter
Lan Nguyen; The Uniform of Death
Relocation
The Natives
A Nisei Picnic

Dwight Okita   208

The Art of Holding On
Crossing with the Light
In Response to Executive Order 9066...
Parachute

Mark Osaki   213

For Avi Killed in Lebanon
Icon
Amnesiac
Turista
Contentment

Richard Oyama   218

The Day After Trinity
Obon By The Hudson
Dreams in Progress
This Song Shows Me Pictures: Morningside Drive, New York City

Al Robles   226

Sushi-Okashi and Green Tea with Mitsu Yashima
Manong Federico Delos Reyes And His Golden Banjo
Manong Jacincto Santo Tomas
Boyang The Wandering Recluse
A Mountain-Toilet Thief

Cathy Song   232

Lucky
Who Makes the Journey
The Day You are Born
Losing Track

Luis Syquia   239

Pan-Asian Holiday Tour
The New Manong

Arthur Sze   244

Moenkopi
Dazzled
Black Lightning
The Cloud Chamber
The Chance
Magnetized

Jeff Tagami   249

Stonehouse
Without Names
Now It's Broccoli
The Foreman's Wife
The Horn Blow

Ronald P. Tanaka   258

The big trimmer
snacks

Kitty Tsui   262

it's in the name
chinatown talking story

George Uba   269

Old Photo, 1942
Gary Gotow
How Do You Spell Missile
Firefly

Nellie Wong   274

Funeral Song for Mamie Eisenhower
Under Our Own Wings
Song of Farewell
New Romance

Shawn Wong   279

An Island
Periods of Adjustment
Lapis

Merle Woo   283

Poems for the Creative Writing Class, Spring 1982
The Subversive
Yellow Woman Speaks

Traise Yamamoto   287

Prelude
In the Van Gogh Room
Diving for Pearls
Biting Through

Cyn. Zarco   292

lolo died yesterday ...
Saxophonetyx
Teaching Poetry
What The Rooster Does Before Mounting

PREFACE

The United States is a nation of many nations. One of the reasons for the vitality of contemporary writing in this country is that incredible diversity of cultures which makes up the mosaic of American life. Yet those parts of the heritage of our literature which stem from Europe are those most often acknowledged and celebrated, even though the contemporary generation of well-known United States writers of European ancestry has felt free to draw extensively on the cultures of Asia and the American Indian (in particular). Many are familiar with the influence of the literary traditions of China upon Ezra Pound, and more than one well-known contemporary American poet has traced his or her "inspirational ancestry" to the Far East. Ironically, this has happened in a nation which has gone through several periods of xenophobic animosity towards that same part of the world and whose last three major wars have been contested wholly or in large part on Asian soil. It is also only in the last few years that we have begun, perhaps, to face up as a nation to the tremendous wrong which was done to Japanese Americans during the Second World War. Many of the voices in this anthology refer directly to those concentration camps which they and their families were forced into for the duration of the war. The first collection of poems by a Japanese American to be published in book form was Lawson Inada's powerful collection *BEFORE THE WAR poems as they-happened* which appeared in 1971.

The images of Asian Americans in Hollywood film and popular books have tended towards the ridiculous, the exotic, and the sinister, from Fu Manchu and Charlie Chan to Suzie Wong. As is the case with all racial stereotyping, it has been a denial of the real humanity of the people seen through that distorted lens. Thanks to such magazines as *Bridge* (32 East Broadway, NYC 10002, which is preparing a literary issue, Vol. 8 no. 4, scheduled for the end of 1983, edited by Walter Lew, with Kimiko Hahn assisting and the fiction edited by Shanlon Wu) such outspoken and courageous artists as the playwright Frank Chin, and such anthologies as *Yardbird Reader*, Vol. 3, edited by Frank Chin and Shawn Wong, *Aiiieeeee!* (Howard University Press), AMERICAN BORN AND FOREIGN (a 1979 special issue of *Sunbury, a poetry magazine*, guest-edited by Fay Chiang, Helen Wong Huie, Jason Hwang, Richard Oyama, and Susan L. Yung), and the Canadian anthology *PAPER DOORS, an anthology of japanese-canadian poetry* (edited by Gerry Shikitani and David Aylward and published by the Coach House Press in 1981), some small amount of attention is finally being focussed upon the unusually good creative writing being done by Asian Americans. At the time of this writing, further publications including a special issue of *Contact II*, co-edited by Laureen Mar, poetry editor, Alan Lau, book review editor, and Jaime Jacinto, Victoria Sales and Karen Tei Yamashita (Brazil), Latin American editors and translators, a new anthology of both prose and fiction edited by Frank Chin, Lawson Inada, Jeffrey Paul Chan, and Shawn Wong entitled THE BIG AIIIEEEEE: Asian-American History in Literature (Howard University Press) and an anthology of Asian-Canadian writers are in their final stages prior to publication. Chinese-American, Japanese American, Filipino American, and Korean American writers are speaking for themselves—as individual human beings who have special heritages they can draw upon as *part of* their inspiration as poets, fiction writers, and playwrights. In a few years, the new generation of immigrants from southeast Asia—Thai, Hmong, Vietnamese—may be producing their Jessica Hagedorns, Frank Chins, Lawson Inadas, Laureen Mars.

It is important, too, to realize that writing by Asian Americans existed long before the 1970's. (West End Press for example, has just published IF YOU WANT TO KNOW WHO WE ARE, selected poems, essays and stories by Carlos Bulosan, a Filipino writer whose major work, AMERICA IS IN THE HEART was published in 1946 and who died in Seattle on September 13, 1956.) In response to an earlier draft of this introduction, Lonny Kaneko wrote: *I think there were people writing about their Asian American experiences throughout our history here. I have Camp newspapers with poems by Nisei describing their anger or pain, we have haiku and tanka that were published in those same newspapers (*Amerasia *printed a group of translators which, when put together as a group read as a trouching story of immigration and disenchantment).* No-No Boy, *of course. And even earlier, the writings of Chinese at Angel Island.*

I was consciously writing about my camp memories in 1961, but could never get those poems published and later made them part of a short story (they were pretty prosy anyway) and several other poems I've since had published were begun in the mid-60's.

I wonder if we seemed quiet only because there was no one around to hear. True, until recently we haven't appeared to have many writers, but the elders have been involved in making life palatable for their families, and while some of our parents may have stressed assimilation, as I look back now, I'm sure that was a product of their survival instinct.

What I'm trying to say is that with the advent of the Aiiieeeee Boys, Amerasia, Greenfield Review, *and* Bridge, *there opened up a body of listeners and readers who had space on their blank pages for Asian American work. Of course there have been stylistic influences from the 60's and the Civil Rights and Women's movements. But I think the* words *have always been there, so have the feelings and ideas behind the words.*

In the spring of 1977, *The Greenfield Review* published a Special Asian American Writers Issue. It was guest-edited by Garrett Kaoru Hongo and no other issue in our fourteen year history as a magazine sold out as quickly as that one did. The birth of this anthology can be traced back to that special issue which showed how meaningful the work of a whole galaxy of Asian Americans could be even to a non-Asian American such as myself.

In a way, this is an outsider's view of contemporary Asian American poetry. I solicited work from more than 200 individual poets, and notices about this anthology appeared in Asian American publications throughout the United States and Canada. We were flooded by submissions. It introduced me to dozens of strong writers whose names and work were unfamiliar. My choices were subjective—I picked the poems I liked best with an eye for variety and giving each poet enough space to give the reader a good taste of his or her work. Hopefully, it will leave you hungry for more. I have chosen the title, BREAKING SILENCE, from a powerful poem by one of the contributors to this anthology, Janice Mirikitani. It exemplifies what I feel is happening with Asian American writers in the United States and Canada (the two nations from which I obtained that sea of submissions and from which I have selected 50 poets). They are adding to the literature and life of their nations and the world, breaking both silence and stereotypes with the affirmation of new songs.

Kikas: Planting Month 1983
Joseph Bruchac
Greenfield Center, N.Y.

A special word of thanks to both Garrett Kaoru Hongo and Alan Chong Lau, both of whom I asked to co-edit this anthology. Instead of co-editing, they gave me help and suggestions which were invaluable. Alan Chong Lau, in particular, gave me the names and addresses of most of the poets I contacted for work and continually has given me guidance along the way to the manuscript's completion, doing more work than most Advisory Editors would do but refusing to accept any of the credit. Thanks also to Laureen Mar, Lonny Kaneko and Fay Chiang for their input—and for the work they continue to do.

Mei-mei Berssenbrugge

Mei-Mei Berssenbrugge was born in 1947 in Peking, China and grew up in Massachusetts. A graduate of Reed College and Columbia University, where she received her MFA, she has received numerous awards for her writing. These include two NEA Grants for literature and the Before Columbus American Book Award. Represented in many magazines and anthologies, her other published collections include PACKRAT SEIVE from Contact II, RANDOM POSSESSION from I. Reed Books, and THE HEAT BIRD from Burning Deck Press. She has worked as an Artist-in-Residence with Basement Workshop and Arts Alaska. From 1977 to the present, she has worked as a Poet-in-the Schools in the state of New Mexico. A Member of the Literature Panel of the New Mexico Arts Commission and the Board of Tooth of Time Press, she is currently living in El Rito, New Mexico.

Farolita

Take a strip of white paper, turn
the top of the strip in your right hand so
it faces the floor, then glue the ends together
If you go along on the outside, it seems
I am not connected to you. I'm trying
to think now if it has to be white paper
Can it show some light through?

It seems I go out on it without any door, into
blue hatchings by yellow grass on snow. This time
of year the air is blue, or inside a shadow. How did she
get through the wall? He was standing at the door waiting
for her. She stands in the field at dusk wearing a black cowboy
hat. She's afraid she becomes something bad at night. She
dreams of killing him, then thinks it is a story she read
She dreams what is going to happen to him. The blue is a false trail
She knows that it is an emanation of the real cloth
The blue mountain is light through fouled air. The blue
air is left after sucking the light

They told her there was a morada across from her house
just a little up from the Kents. She never wanted to go
there. In a magazine its long Christ held flowers
and an ax. Toward town, in low sun, she sees light
in flapping laundry. It was just movement at first. She has
heard the processions walk by. At first you think their
singing is a moan in the wind. He too makes a ritual
out of holding her breasts to cold glass. She thinks someone is
stealing her black cigarettes. She considers its madonna
a kind of barker, or an emanation of scored flesh. The
yellow grass has nevertheless been trampled by cows
and turns to mud, though nothing was green there, before
A white cloth tears off in the wind and flattens itself
against a fence, holding shadows the way black plastic holds
little hands of water in its folds on the field

I am talking about the color white. Please don't try to make
me think I have not murdered you in my dream. He is taking
her to a dinner party across the road. An artist tells
her about a film he conceived, that is all one color, the
color inside a shadow. She tries not to assume this is
because he is going blind. She loves him. He is a capitalist
Sparks shot out the chimney and streaked outside the glass
wall like an opened lens on their cigarettes in the dark. One
log burning heated the vast room. The whole wall was hot
to touch. She folded each napkin so its white bird flew off
to the left. Each fish leapt off white on the Japanese
plates. Her host's sculptures had undergone amputations
They'd been hung by their wrists from a beam, but were
all smooth now. She drank some vodka and ice. The ice
which had been refrozen, held little bubbles in the act

of rising that were half light. She realized it was
time to go attach herself, at home

Trying to tell me it is every color, that is their way
of drawing you in. Keep your eye on the leaf dangling
from a bare branch. It is dead, but is moving and
seems to have candlelight on it, though when white
chrysanthemums arrived, she couldn't help accepting
She told her mother they were from George. Her mother
told all the neighbors. They wanted her to marry
She thought she was pregnant. She wondered if paper were
suitable for its clothes, so she pretended to make patterns
for the clothes, but they *were* the clothes

White light from her fingers, I think it is
electricity leaking from the wall, but it washes back
from hitting the wall. I demeaned myself in front of a
blind man, because I'm afraid of myself at night. If
he lights my cigarette when I complain how it goes out, the
flame goes out. I am afraid I might drop my bag and
secretly scoop the used matches up. It ricochets from a
box canyon. It doesn't recognize her as it strikes, so
she is visible, too. The whole valley becomes a white
bowl. The phosphorus wedge of a police car over-
exposes outlines of her friends. They'd been passing
a bottle of Merseault inside the pick-up. They told her
not to sit there like a wooden doll answering his personal
questions. She grew confused. She tried to draw in her cape
She walked a little away and rolled over on the snow
Her foot became a horse's head in the fire

The Eurasian at the party would not speak to her. Little lights
inside paper sacks cast willow flames on the snow
the little lights that line paths
of the courtyard. You have to assume each is the same, so
the maze recedes and is not a vertical map of varying sacks
on a blank wall, since it is dark, oh
Mei-mei, you've walked in that garden before. I'm sick of
these dry gardens. Everyone tells me I should get angry at him
The nun's voice quavered behind a screen. There was a shadow
voice to hers of another one singing quietly and
a little off. I prefer to think it was the light back
How can he dream of tying me to his bed, in a blizzard
with snow to my thigh? He tells me I am flirting
with the void. I am not Chinese. I invite him to step
out to the garden for plum blossoms. They would be
very beautiful, now. Their petals would
blanket the snow like snow on sand
but it is morning

Open the door
Light falls like a collar point on the blond floor boards
She crosses this point, and light falls on her
and it falls on her as she goes out
but it is different light

Luis Cabalquinto

Born in Magarao, Camarines Sur, Philippines. Currently studying with Galway Kinnell in the graduate program in creative writing at New York University, New York City. Works as an editor at Pfizer International, New York Headquarters. Won an Academy of American Poets poetry prize in 1982 (New York University). Winner of the 1978 Dylan Thomas Poetry Award from the New School for Social Research, New York City. Studied at Cornell University, University of the Philippines, Ateneo de Naga (Naga City, Philippines) Attended writing workshops and conferences at Bread Loaf, Vermont; Silliman University; University of the Philippines; Writers' Community (New York City; New School (New York City); 92nd St. Y Poetry Center (New York City); Cornell University (Ithaca, N.Y.). Poetry anthologized in: "American Born & Foreign: An Anthology of Asian-American Poetry" (1979, U.S.); "An Anthology of Poems 1965-1974" (Philippines); "An Anthology of Erotic Poetry" (forthcoming U.S. publication). Published poems in American Poetry Review, New American & Canadian Poetry, Sunbury Magazine, Trojan Horse, Alkahest, Junction, Poetry Australia, Manila Review, Folio, Solidarity, Focus Philippines, Likhaan, Pamana, Panorama, Expressweek Magazine, Bridge, *and* Greenfield Review.

4

Blue Tropic

(for Mariflor Parpan)

In May
Back in the Islands
When the days are women
    without men
And the nights are wrapped
    around us
    like a womb
We would sit on the grass
    or on wicker chairs
    or on long wooden benches
And look at the moon rising
    or, without a moon
    the brilliant
    stars
We would talk, our voices
    harmonized
    with the hum
    of the evening
The chirp of a sleepless sparrow
    roosting in a tree
    the ringing of a cricket
And the distant thunder of trucks going North
Then the land of China would belong
    to China
And America would belong to America
The rest of Asia and Africa and Europe
    would be
    in their chosen
    places
And in the islands named The Philippines
In a town called Magarao
In the yard of my ancestral home
    my brothers and sisters and I
    my mother and I
Would be gathered for an evening's miracle
    the summer's satori
That even if tomorrow the crops should fail
A war be declared
Or a death in the family occur
    only this moment's knowledge
    only this closeness to kin
To bird and cricket and grass and tree
And to stars or moon and trucks heading North
    and to my mother
    only this alignment
    should matter

Luis Cabalquinto   5

The Flower Vendor

(for Nick Joaquin)

The woman was heavy with child:
But this was not the reason
Which moved us to buy
All her jasmine flowers at her price,

As we sat in the car waiting
For the light to change in Cubao.*
It was the face of her thin head
With wispy hair that seemed to float

In the city sun and summer wind
That took us. And the deep
Brown eyes that seemed to fill
With the sadness of a city

And a lifetime. When she handed
Us the strings of white flowers and
Took our bill she smiled: so
Swiftly did that small face change.

But the traffic signals turned from red to green
And the light in us went from stop to go.

*a Philippine city just outside Manila.

The Big One

I like to fish,
an old habit,
for a definition
outside
the act itself:
in addition to
the useful air
and exercise.

The lake will do
without
my best mono:
the star-drag reel,
lures of the trade,
and rod. Or lines.

I go for the clipped lift,
the sudden suck,
caught in the teeth
of sky and water—
the trembling stop
of bait in a
sudden shift
of scale:
struck by bass!
in the brain.

Eating Lechon, with my brothers and sisters

(For George Lai)

What fullness in the life is this which possesses
An October night
In the patio of my mother's house
Eating lechon with my brothers & sisters
At a reunion —
We laugh, we dine & wine: my nephews I don't recognize—
Grown: my nieces beautiful, with smooth skins &
White teeth: against my brothers' & sisters' dark
Middle age.
They are all here, all ears:
I tell them about the Flamenco dancers in Madrid;
How the lights bloom each night in Paris;
How cold the lakes are in September in Switzerland;
I tell them about my disappointments in Rome; how I danced
All night with friends on a canal barge in Amsterdam
Where they served the best wine & cheese.
I tell them, too, about the poverty I saw in India
& the beauty of the Taj. And I tell them specially
About the Chinese friend I met in London & seen again
In Hongkong: the surprising hospitality: the nights
At the Chinese opera: the endless dinners: the eating
With chopsticks in the cold blue dawn at a sidewalk table
In a secret quarter in Kowloon where old men sleep on
Doorsteps.
They are here, they listen.
We all listen, late into the night in the light of
A full moon over Magarao. We dream our dreams
Again: brothers & sisters, nephews & nieces, mother
& siblings: together.
Later, as I rest alone in my room, hearing
My nieces sing of love & the adolescent
In the dulcet tone of my childhood dialect,
I also hear a silence beyond their young
Voices, undisturbed but for the bark of a dog.
I listen & try to take all in
With a new understanding.
When sleep comes gently
I feel at peace: tonight at least, content.

Hometown

After a supper of mountain rice
And wood-roasted river crab
I sit on a long bench outside
The old house, looking at a river

Alone, myself, again away
From that other self in the city
On this piece of ancestor land
My pulses slowed, I am at peace

I have no wish but this place
To remain here in a stopped time
With stars moving on that water
And in the sky a brightness

Answering: I want nothing else
But this stillness filling me
From a pure darkness over the hand
That smells ever freshly of trees

The night and I are quiet now
But for small laughter from a neighbor
The quick sweep of a winged creature
And a warm dog, snuggled by my feet

Virginia Cerenio

Virginia R. Cerenio is a 2nd-generation FilipinoAmerican who grew up in San Francisco. She received her education at San Francisco State University, earning a B.A. in English, a teaching credential, and is presently completing an M.A. in Second Language Acquisition and Cross-Cultural Education. She has worked as a teacher and curriculum writer. Her poetry has appeared in Liwanag, Women Talking-Women Listening, Bridge Magazine and will be appearing in Greenfield Review and East Wind Magazine. An upcoming issue of Berkeley Fiction Review will print a short story. She is also a member of Kearny Street Workshop.

> "Writing is a fusion of art & politics; a tool for capturing those emotions that can only be imagined between the lines in history books. Anger cannot make poems, it is the beauty of the expression of anger that makes poems. In crafting a writing style, I seek to contain the tension and balance between art & politics."

you lovely people

we are a lovely people
we flamenco our way
thru the heart of america
w/o missing a beat

like indios, we are
lost
not in india or middle america
or the wrong side of a carabao nickel
but on a boat
    between oceans
    between continents
indios
on spanish galleons
to new orleans
revolutionary pirates
schoolboy cooks
militant farmworkers
pineapple canners
fish piecers
gold miners
navy shoeshiners
poolhall hustlers
now we are all manongs

ay, manong
your old brown hands
hold life, many lives
within each crack
a story

pinay

blue
on
blue
denim poverty
snapping gum in time to de wonder of stevie wonder
street music can salsa your soul away
armed with a hairbrush n the static electricity of youth
shy smile like the promise of rivers in a tropical jungle
she wears america like one pair of blue jeans after another
but the blue waters of manila bay wet her eyes shine her lips
songcry of rainbirds escape her teeth
the sun does a spanish tango in her hair
    like a flock of blue-jeaned birds
    feathered n fluffed
    they preen themselves at the bus stop
    twittering exitement in crystalsmooth notes
    fly away one after the other
    like stars blinking at the dawn

pick-up at chef rizal restaurant

a young pinoy
he
like a dark alley
too quiet
        w/his brushed back hair
        leathered jacket
        ben davis pants
        w/ his nikes on
stepping too quiet
        he plays pinball
        hands dancing to lights n bells
        but his hips rest silently against the machine.
he orders chicken adobo over rice
his mouth lingers with pleasure
swallows food like a starving man
but his eyes do not say anything
only silently dart to each corner of the room
like a nervous billiard ball
before falling in the hole
running again to hide
in the corner pockets in back of his head
        he wipes his sleeve against his mouth
        sitting back with a puppet's jerk
        watching the white man
        with the slightly balding head
        pay the pretty pinay behind the counter
        "two plates chicken adobo and rice"
        the young pinoy follows him out
        shoulders hunched against questions
        from the silent brown eyes watching him
        silence only broken
        by rizal weeping verses

manong benny

his gentle heart shows through
sunlight eyes
his bamboo bones
knobbed at every joint
he sways   laughing
flute-songs at every breeze.
he writes letters laced with thankyous
"i appreciate your very kind hearted visited me
while i am a sickly poor man as you've seen me"
his camera hold helicopters
n hot air balloons in constant flight
with his eyes closed   he bends his body
into the wind   riding waves of air
like a kite   flying   always flying
over kearny st rice terraces
circling manilatown n the pyramid
forcasting spring rains
n the children laughing in his wake

we who carry the endless seasons
   of tropical rain in our blood
still weep our mother's tears
feel the pain of their birth
        their growing
          as women in america

we wear guilt for their minor sins
              singing lullabies
              in foreign tongue
                   ". . . o ilaw sa gabing madilim
                   wangis mo'y bituin sa langit . . ."
      their desires
              wanting us
              their daughters
              to marry only
                   ". . . a boy from the islands . .
                   ang guapo lalake . . . and
                   from a good family too. . . ."
  like shadows
  attached to our feet
  we cannot walk away

though we are oceans and dreams apart
waves carry the constant clicking of their rosary beads
                   like heartbeats
                   in our every breathing

Photo by Anne Sager

Diana Chang

While my main concerns in my novels seem to be in character, emotion and being, in my poetry I often write of the land, the ocean, the moon. Is it because they are less mortal than I, and keep me in touch with the eternal? Of course, I have other themes too: the word itself; love or love manqué; creativity and art.

My poetry has been described by Shirley Lim, critic-poet, as that "of a persona so elusive and fragile that we have a sense of endless secrecy, of the utmost intimate eavesdropping." Dexter Fisher, anthologist-editor, said, "Her use of understatement lends an element of surprise to her poetry as well as a resonance that goes beyond the subject."

That I am also a painter is reflected in my writing, I believe, which is imagistic, and my drawings and paintings are included in the collections of James Brooks, Alfonso Ossorio, and Betty Friedan, among others.

At Barnard College, I teach creative writing in the English Department and a course, "Imagery and Form in the Arts", in the Program in the Arts.

The titles of my six novels in the order of their appearance are:

The Frontiers of Love *Random House (Frederick Muller and Ace Books in England)*

A Woman of Thirty *Random House (Frassinelli in Italy)*

A Passion for Life *Random House and Bantam Books (W.H. Allen in England)*

The Only Game in Town *Signet original, New American Library*

Eye to Eye *Harper & Row*

A Perfect Love *Jove Books (subsidiary of Harcourt Brace Jovanovich)*

My poetry, The Horizon Is Definitely Speaking, *came out in June, 1982 in a volume published by Backstreet Editions, Street Press, and co-funded by the National Endowment for the Arts.*

16

Artists East and West

Buson, Goshun, Kinkoku,
Japanese of the eighteenth century,
painted Vermont snow, old and fresh

their squatting poets fool other rocks
their stones think like men

find their movement
in ways like Motherwell

or Renoir, closer to Fifth Avenue
his sweet, short faces
and ephemeral arms

whispering of monumentality

Kokoschka and Klimt
say hello through Buson and circle

massing energies

in our neighborhood
we dream in white and black
along lines
they leave

The Horizon is Definitely Speaking

When clouds inch
     and the hill stays

what are we to know?

Geese overhead
     chew the fat all the way
Trees like wishbones
     are nested with knowledge

I stare into a bush
     until I become secrets, too

All around, suggestions
     that the sky is in pieces at our feet

the water is too still
and we are on edge

Once and Future

In China they have ghost chairs
Time sits in them
and on its lap rocks the vanished
     forever gathering up the worn

When I took home an old bed frame
from a legacy in Wainscott
I thought of those ancestor thrones

I stepped in and out of the bed
as if it were a courtyard
     a wing for new cousins

I stood a lamp within it
Watched the ghost light
carol for body upon body

who circle for safe landings
out of the dark

to continue arrivals of the young

Codes

An undulation
on too many legs
crossing the path
in such a manner as to suggest
it would blush if it were noticed

Is a cat.

These people
who have still to stop smiling and be introduced
might move you to cry out

If you knew their names.

A lack of words feels like dusk:
We are not blind but we are uncertain we see.

Its pain is matched
by this other remorse for names

Which bring them to mind truly,
falsely —

mountains
women
fish

Second Nature

How do I feel
Fine wrist to small feet?
I cough Chinese.

To me, it occurs that Cezanne
Is not a Sung painter.

(My condition is no less gratuitous than this remark.)

The old China muses through me.
I am foreign to the new.
I sleep upon dead years.

Sometimes I dream in Chinese.
I dream my father's dreams.

I wake, grown up
And someone else.

I am the thin edge I sit on.
I begin to gray — white and black and in between.
My hair is America.

New England moonlights in me.

I attend what is Chinese
In everyone.

We are in the air.

I shuttle passportless within myself,
My eyes slant around both hemispheres,
Gaze through walls

And long still to be
Accustomed,
At home here,

Strange to say.

Fay Chiang

Fay Chiang is a writer and visual artist living in New York's Lower East Side. Since 1971, she has worked with other Asian American artists at the Basement Workshop, a cultural arts organization with programs in the literary, visual and performing arts. Her poetry has appeared in the following anthologies: American Born and Foreign (Sunbury Press), Ordinary Woman (Ordinary Women Books), The Third Woman (Houghton Mifflin), as well as in Essence Magazine, Greenfield Review and Ikon. Her two volumes of poetry were published by Sunbury Press: In The City of Contradictions (1979), and Miwa's Song (1982). Ms. Chiang received a CAPS: Poetry grant in 1982.

Presently she is working on a full length play, "Laundryman," commissioned by the New York Chinatown History Project; a children's book and rehearsing "Trilogy"—a three section adaptation of her poetry—for performance with actress Mary Lum.

Snow

snow falls in a hush under night lights, lampposts
doing waltzes.

I feel hopeful, though logic says to worry. we run
out of money with budget cuts in the arts, in
unemployment, food stamps, medicaid, housing. we've
got two hands apiece, we'll figure something out.

it snows now. tops of buildings covered white
and figures walking slowly past drifts on streets
below. pure spirits smokelike float on each snowflake
searching for kin.

put away the papers, stack the work for tomorrow,
turn the calendar page. each time the ritual
prepares for a new beginning. I walk slowly down
seven flights of darkened wooden stairs, past
other lofts filled with oiled machinery for small
industries. the front door opens and my coat is
caught by chill seeping through a hole in the
right pocket. shuddering I walk towards spring
street, past the iron security gates of the
carpenter, the chinese family coffee shop, the
rice and beans restaurant, the corner smoke shop.
people have gone home. they must be eating supper,
maybe watching t.v. or preparing a sandwich to
take to work, school. or maybe sick in bed with
this flu.

down spring street there are silent side streets,
loading bays scattered in snow, by workers
hurrying home at 5 p.m. windows reflect snow,
lamplight. they are eyes. I look past instead
staring skyward and search the darkness for
the source of this snow. but there are many
snowflakes and they swirl in patterns like
messengers, their secrets entwined in one
another, my figure swept up by their dances,
in motion.

I am excited: a warm glow in my chest expanding,
breathing. there is a song about living, about
being. I hear it when I walk through snow
under lamplight in city streets.

A Letter to Peter

got your note today and I'm glad you wrote.
snowing all day, getting lost in between
snowflakes when I go by windows in the loft.

when I'm lost in plans about coming out to
san francisco, it's like a song: pure singing of
a note clean as rain. I'm really excited; so
is jean. ma wants to stay home, I think to get
used to being by herself and to have some of
her friends over. there's a growing chinese
community within a radius of five blocks around
our house and the mothers bring their babies
and little kids to visit ma and bobo.

maybe she'll come out in the spring, see all
the relatives in the bay area.

there's been an incredible amount of junk in
the house to clear out: old clothes, too much
furniture, books, the inventory of a family's
life. walking around in a puzzle trying to
figure out what is essential for posterity.

sometimes I walk around the house and miss
you. the first few days after you went west,
jean and I would come home and think you
were still in your room. the leavings take
time to register. we'll have a good time
and catch up when we visit. is it warm now
in san francisco? I want to watch clouds roll
blending like a jewel smoothed by time.

it isn't easy these changes in the family,
life, in me. sometimes I walk around the city
catching stone lions on 42nd or wake from
dreams that slip away.

I do feel a trust in what is happening, though
I do not understand it all.

see you soon. love, fay   1/17/78

Voices That Have Filled My Day

dreaming you say thank you
I ask thank you for what?

someone yells hector!
    hey julio! hector! julio!
    no one is home

a breeze faint slides
pass curtains
hells angels gun bikes
down third towards the river
a window opens
conversation drifts upstairs
I can't hear what
they are saying

this sultry city night
recalls voices
that have filled my day

Mercedes is home from Toronto
    you know about family
    when you're away from them
    you miss them
    when you're with them
    you want to get away
    if ever understood
    it's the stuff
    to all great stories

at the office
    Teddy and I work through
    mailing lists
    picking and sorting
    names like seeds and burrs
    carding from fiber
    spinning thread to weave
        a new season

in a magazine, a woman potter says
    I work for a life
        not of money and success
    but a life
        of human freedom and dignity

I meet Tomomi
    Jean met Tomomi in a hallway
    in San Miguel de Allende
    students at the university
        Jean digging clay
            from the Mexican earth
            hauling it to work
                with her hands

spinning the wheel
with her legs
back bent, hands raising
deftly wet, clean forms
shaping a life
Tomomi traveling and living
in villages and homes
of native artisans, weavers
learning the art of
backstrap weaving
gathering, drying, grinding
the humble cochineal bug
brewing and testing
its dyes over a boiling pot
open fire
steam rising like mist
at morning over Mt. Fuji
their roads cross
for a moment
then hold

we have coffee at Kate's
who has been to Calcutta
seeing poverty unbearable
except for those within it
whose belief in the afterlife
negates the presence
of cholera streaming
from infested English barracks
on the hill, by the mouth
of the stream
feeding the city's thirst
outraged, Kate storms
to the Health Department
he says why bother
saving them from cholera
if they will then die
from malnutrition
here in India
it all evens out

Peter gets better in the hospital
memories fading of a past
once catching his footsteps
and taking away the sound
over the telephone
he asks if I couldn't bring
some change, magazines, fruits
I bring them tomorrow
we make plans to take a walk

we sit in a coffee shop in Chinatown
Meimei says I've begun to collect
bones for you and

I will lend you the
beautiful horse skull
someone has given me
parched by sun on desert floor
by brush, by cacti

my house is adobe
  with a tin roof
  a wood eating stove
  fed by the woodpile
  a ways from the water pump
Teddy talks about light
shafts of available light
 in a four foot square
 in a darkened space
 of a dance she travels in
     with sounds
       of chopping wood
       water dripping from a faucet
       her own breathing
       the turning of a page
  we talk about movements
  in the universe
  and light, natural light
  the scale of all these things
  around us wonderingly

in this darkened kitchen
  I recall dreams from a decade ago
    dreams like stars
      some fixed in constellations
      others bursting like comets
      fiery, sudden, gone

  down the hall
  someone unlocks a door
  they've come home

  I thank you for the sunrise

Photo by Maggie Dusheko

Marilyn Chin

Marilyn Chin is a poet and translator who is presently living in California. She is a graduate of the Iowa Writer's Workshop and was a translator for the International Writing Program at the University of Iowa. Her work has appeared in a variety of literary journals and anthologies, namely, "Massachusetts Review", "Iowa Review", "Kayak", "Seneca Review", "Writer's Forum", "Modern Poetry in Translation", 100 Contemporary poets (edited by David Ray for Sparrow Press) and others. This selection is from her soon-to-be completed manuscript Dwarf Bamboo.

Write, Do Write

for Ai Qing

It was Pablo who saw him most clearly—
"Miguel, with a face of a potato plucked from the earth."
If there was a boy with roots still showing,
seedy-faced and dirt in his nostrils,
it was Miguel Hernandez, scooped, gouged, wrested
from his peasant's earth.

But, as I walked closer, I saw
the plum white body of a smooth turnip
scrubbed and fragrant, with tufts of baby-fine hair...
it was James Wright who was one day pulled
from his Ohio soil to bake in the kitchens of America.

Tonight, all of poetry lowers its head
for those who died so we might live. And now...

A message to the impoverished poet in New York,
a poet who has been feeding himself macaroni on dirty forks—
what is your struggle? The rent, the whiskey,
your personal apocalypse: the woman no longer loves you
for you are a beast.

And to you, the exiled one in Singkiang, waiting twenty years
for the sun,
a large, hideous lantern strutting
over the barbarian wilderness—

Wherever you are, don't forget me, please—
on heaven's stationary, with earth's chalk,
write, do write.

Grandmother Poems

1.
My grandmother is old, not old
like Tu Fu, the Yangtze, Beijing,
they are old forever.
My grandmother is old, weathermauled
by five thousand years of love and torrential rain.
And Hsing Hsing is a child of hers,
Not like Sung Mei Ling or Chiang Ch'ing,
daughters of silk, wives of generals—
Hsing Hsing is the last glimmer.

And I am a child of theirs, born, January,
to a man in black, king of dogs and Mah Jong,
who slapped the I-ching on the table . . .
Year of the Goat, sign of earth, chert and grief,
      death by fire.

2.
Burmese is a bright green jade.
My grandmother wore it to her deathbed.
My mother did not.
I wear it in shape of an oblong heart
on a gold chain around my neck.
Cousins in blue jeans point at my throat,
"A Chinese woman doesn't wear jade,
only ricebags, buckets, hoes,
scythes and hemp-made clothes."

"Cousins, heart and spleen aren't red but green.
Not love but hate brings you here.
Not blood nor kin but envy.
Beauty is all a woman needs on earth,
Beauty—and we ain't many."

3.
Mother was the cross
mulish woman, who scrubbed her house bald.
Her floor, her child
must be clean, clean to impress.
Now the soap still sticks to the ceiling
of my mouth; what I say leaks out of the small apse
of my heart. They are all dead, my mother's half.
Who will marry me, the clean eyesore of spring?

Auntie Jade with the fat green face, the only one alive,.
squats me in front of the mirror,
winds my hair up into a beehive,
"Be prepared to meet thy tall dark savior!"

Grandmother, tomorrow I must anoint my head
in white, the color of mourning,
white, the pallor of the dead.

The Landlord's Wife

I still have a sister in Guang Dung.
I know this; she sends photographs.
And a scholar-of-a-brother in Beijing
Thrown to the academic pigs.
And you, Chao Zhi, straddling
The three forked rivers of Pittsburgh,
Write only once a dull spring
On scarlet or crimson origami
And never green or blue.
With which folded tongue did you say
"I loved you," with whose?

*   *   *

December 12, 1919,
The village's smallest boy
Displayed your head on the crags.
What could have bound us together then,
The blood, the wrath ... our children?
The poor who tried to read your intents,
Your downturned mouth—
Should I have told them north,
When you had always said south?

Their austere leader, lord
Of the land, who "never lied,"
Always lied, heart severed from head.
Still, that pride was embossed
On your teeth's gilded grin ...
You squandered their gains
And cursed their losses
As I kept my head bent, embroidering
"Longevity" with red silk thread.

*   *   *

Their running grass, their watery hand—
"Japanese four-legged, traitor-hound."
Once, I was the wealthiest woman in Guang Dung.
Now, I chew bitterroot and a deadman's brine.
Gao, the diviner, always said, "Breathe first, then, breed."
But I was too spoiled to be philosophical.
Now with ten children, five horses,
Enough gold for the distant bandits,
Enough food for half the journey ...

"Let us through, let us through,
I never loved him, never.
The only man I love now, the only man I believe—
The man from above, from Yenan."

Notes:

"Japanese four-legged ..." during the Anti-Japanese Resistence, derogatory name-calling for the Japanese invaders as well as for the Chinese accomplices, mostly wealthy landlords and corrupt officials.

"Running grass"—style of calligraphy.

We Are A Young Nation, Uncle

Old river, once blue-mercurial—
Now lackluster and pale as balm;
The forests and dark alcoves
I remember once
Echoed with tall battles,
Are now driven to the remains of peace:
Burnt fields, dead tallow,
Dry brown dregs of a newborn earth.
Though you keep clutching
Your heart, squawking and honking,
For the old gargoyle, death
Has pressed her body tautly over yours.
We fought the best we could:
Boiled five fingers of ginseng,
Burnt paper coins,
Chanted the Gao Wang Sutra.
But dying men need no money;
What you conquered
Will be divided later—
When your name, that one distinct syllable,
Walks out the door;
When your daughter marries
Into the next village,
Dragging with her
Your last good hen
For the New Year's sacrifice.
Old man, beware,
Ling Ling is marrying a general;
Her pelvis may be ruined
For a thousand years.

A Chinaman's Chance

If you were a Chinese born in America, who would you believe
Plato who said what Socrates said
Or Confucius in his bawdy way:
    "So a male child is born to you
    I am happy, very very happy."

————————

The railroad killed your great-grandfather
His arms here, his legs there . . .
How can we remake ourselves in his image?

Your father worked his knuckles black
So you might have pink cheeks. Your father
Burped you on the back; why must you water his face?

Your father was happy, he was charred by the sun,
Danced and sang until he died at twenty-one.

Lord, don't you like my drinking. Even Jesus
Had a few in his day with Mary before
He gambled his life for us on the cross—

And for us he lost his life, for us.

Your body is growing, changing, running
Away from your soul. Look,

Not a sun but a gold coin at the horizon,
Chase after it, my friend, after it.

————————

Why does the earth move backwards
As we walk ahead. Why does mother's
Blood stain this hand-me-down shirt?

This brown of old tea, the yellow ring
Around the same porcelain cup. They stayed

Stone-faced as paired lions, prepared
As nightwatch at the frontier gate.

We have come small and wooden, tanned brown
As oak pillars, eyes peering straight
Through vinyl baggage and uprooted shoes.

We shall gather their leftovers: jimsons and velvets,
Crocuses which have burst-bloomed through walks.
We shall shatter this ancient marble, veined and glorious . . .

Little path, golden arrows, could you pave
My future in another child's neighborhood?

Night: black starred canopy, piece
Of Chinese silk, dank with must and cedar,
Pulled down from the source, a cardboard bolt.

Eric Chock

I believe that the point of view I write from is born of the local culture which has developed in Hawaii in the last few decades. I write on various subjects, personal or public, or ideally, a combination of the two, hoping to capture some sense of the various cultural influences which affect individual's lives. I believe in the function that poetry and all art performs in reflecting and shaping the culture which gives it life, which sustains it. I believe that this social function of poetry is part of the give and take between life and art which ideally makes the two indistinguishable, exciting, and mutually beneficial. And I believe that this process is inevitable.

For the last ten years I have enjoyed working in the Hawaii Poets In The Schools program. Since 1978 I have co-edited Bamboo Ridge, The Hawaii Writers' Quarterly, *with Darrell Lum. I have served on the Board of Directors of the Hawaii Literary Arts Council and in 1980 was elected its president. Presently I am a member of the Honolulu City Commission on Culture and the Arts.*

My publications are almost exclusively in Hawaii. I have a collection of poems called Ten Thousand Wishes, *available through the Before Columbus Foundation, 1446 Sixth Street, #D, Berkeley, California, 94710.*

Papio*

This one's for you, Uncle Bill.
I didn't want to club the life
from its blue and silver skin,
so I killed it by holding it
upside-down by the tail
and singing into the sunset.
It squeaked air three times
in a small dying chicken's voice,
and became a stiff curve
like a wave that had frozen
before the break into foam.

In the tidal pool
you used to stand in,
I held the fish and laughed
thinking how you called me
handsome at thirteen.
I slashed the scaled belly,
pulled gills and guts,
and a red flower bloomed
and disappeared with a wave
like the last breath
your body heaved
on a smuggled Lucky Strike and Primo
in a hospital bed.
You wanted your ashes out at sea
but Aunty kept half on the hill.
She can't be swimming the waves at her age
and she wants you still.

*"Papio" is the Hawaiian word for Jack Crevalle, a popular game and food fish.
(pah peé oh)

For The Field

When she opened her eyes the fields were gone into houses. It wasn't so bad they were peopled by strangers, but even her daughters and grandchildren didn't remember the shack with the dirt floor where the chickens came in, scratching. There had been a stream where she washed her face every morning, where she drank from, and where she swam on hot days.

Those days were spent telling stories to boulders, stories the crayfish remembered of cat eyes slanting sharp in the grass; of the desperate whisper of rainbow fish and blue moons fearing the scoop of the red net; of the giant brown catfish with knives in its gills, and you could trade blood with the catch if you liked.

Her audience of rocks listened around the pond, and the water didn't believe her and kept going by. Now the stream runs underground in cement pipes. But the stones are beginning to remember. Buried for so long, they shrug their shoulders and wallow deeper in mud that reminds them of little girl voices on hot days. The strangers' houses shift uneasily. As a little girl goes to the toilet she notices the water, rising in the white bowl. For a minute, she shuts her eyes.

Pulling Weeds

Dirt sticks under fingernails
harder than penny-a-weed,
and my young knuckles ached
pulling against those roots.
I worked hard as you did
(though you earned twice as much),
but so much crabgrass and nutgrass
littered our dream of lawn;
or was that some lesson in survival
through hard work in plantation fields
which you were passing on to me?
No television, no ice cream,
no nickel for candy that rots
teeth quicker than chewing
sugarcane or mangoes.
You gave me your heritage,
keeping dirt in my nails,
a natural taste in my mouth,
and you stood over me
like the white man you hate
in your dreams.

The Mango Tree

"One old Chinese man told me," he said, *"that he like for trim his tree so the thing is hollow like one umbrella, and the mangoes all stay hanging underneath. Then you can see where all the mangoes stay, and you know if ripe. If the branches stay growing all over the place, then no can see the mango, and the thing get ripe, and fall on the ground."*

And us guys, we no eat mango that fall down. Going get soft spots. And always get plenty, so can be choosy. But sometimes, by the end of mango season when hardly get already, and sometimes the wind blow em down, my mother, sometimes she put the fall down kind in the house with the others.

I was thinking about that as I was climbing up the tree. The wind was coming down from the Pali, and I gotta lean into the wind every time she blow hard. My feet get the tingles cause sometimes the thing slip when I try for grip the bark with my toes. How long I never go up that tree! I stay scared the branch going broke cause too small for hold me, and when the wind blow, just like being on one see-saw. And when I start sawing that branch he told me for cut, the thing start for jerk, and hard for hold on with my feet. Plus I holding on to one branch above my head with one hand, and the fingers getting all cramp. My legs getting stiff and every few strokes my sawing arm all tired already, so when the wind blow strong again, I rest. I ride the branch just like one wave. One time when I when look down I saw him with one big smile on his face. Can tell he trying not for laugh.

He getting old but he spend plenty time in that tree. Sometime he climb up for cut one branch and he stay up for one hour, just looking around, figuring out the shape of the tree, what branches for cut and what not for cut. And from up there can see the whole valley. Can see the trees and the blue mountains. I used to have nightmares that the thing was going erupt and flood us out with lava, and I used to run around looking for my girlfriend so she could go with our family in our '50 Dodge when we run away to the ocean. But I never find her and I got lost. Only could see smoke, and people screaming, and the lava coming down.

The nightmare everytime end the same. I stay trapped on one trail in the mountains, right on one cliff. Me and some guys. The trail was narrow so we walking single file. Some people carrying stuff, and my mother in front of me, she carrying some things wrapped in one cloth. One time she slip, and I grab for her, and she starting for fall and I scream "Oh no!" and then I wake up. And I look out my window at the mango tree and the blue mountains up the valley. The first time I when dream this dream I was nine.

Since that time I when dream plenty guys falling off the trail. And plenty times I when grab for my mother's hand when she start for fall. But I never fall. I still stay lost on the cliff with the other guys. I still alive.

And my father still sitting in the mango tree just like one lookout, watching for me and my mother to come walking out of the mountain. Or maybe he stay listening to the pali wind for the sound one lady make if she falls. Or maybe he just sitting in his mango tree umbrella, rocking like one baby in the breeze, getting ripe where we can see him. And he's making sure no more extra branches getting in the way.

*"Pali" is Hawaiian for cliff or steep mountain. On Oahu the "Pali" is a reference to the pass connecting Honolulu (the city side) with the Windward (or country) side of the island. (pah'lee)

Termites

On summer nights they swarm.
They seem to come out of the ground,
out of trees, they fill the air.
They wander down the streets,
wings glittering under streetlights.
They've kept these wings
all their lives
folded on their backs,
but in these insect starbursts
they fly toward whatever shines
in streetlights, headlights,
reflections in windows, or eyes.

We turn off the lights inside.
We watch as toads
gather at the porch light
and lick themselves silly.
Lizards haunt the windows,
stalking the winged or wingless bodies.
Sometimes they remain stationary,
content to eat what rushes past
the half-inch reach of their roll-up tongues.
If the creatures get in
we have candles flaming,
or white bowls of hot water
grandma leaves under a lamp
in a darkened room.
Looking out from the window,
it seems as though they're all bent
on living in our home.

Every summer they swarm.
Thousands.
Like drunken tourists
lost on New Year's Eve.
But in twenty minutes
their eyes are glazed with the glare of light,
their craziness for it so rapidly reversed,
and once again they crawl
for tunnels, baseboards,
any dark opening they can find.
On summer nights, thousands of wings
form feathery wreaths around each house.
Some of these have made it.
But out in front under the streetlight
mother shoots water like a gunner,
picking off stragglers
with the garden hose.

Cyril Dabydeen

South American born (from Guyana) poet and short story writer, Cyril Dabydeen has won the Sandbach Parker Gold Medal, the highest poetry award in his native country, before he was twenty. He received his post-graduate degrees at Queen's University in Canada, and has devoted much of his time to writing. He has published six books of poetry, and one of short stories. His poetry and short stories have appeared in nearly all the major literary magazine in Canada; and he has also appeared in the magazines in W. Germany, the U.S.A., the Caribbean, Denmark, India, etc.

He has done extensive readings of his work across Canada, and is actively involved in the Asian and West Indian literary and ethnic scene held on this subject in Canada. He presented a paper in Havana, Cuba (most recently); and is scheduled to do a reading at the University of Iowa in the Fall. He is editing an anthology of Asian-Canadian poetry.

His books include: Distances *(Fiddlehead Press),* Goatsong *(Mosaic Press),* Heart's Frame *(Vesta Publications)* This Planet Earth *(Borealis Press),* Elephants Make Good Stepladders *(Third Eye Publication); and* Still Close to the Island *(stories) Commoners' Press)*

He is currently working on a number of other poetry and short story collections, as well as on a novel.

Folklore

This is my legacy.
Sugar. Sun and topsoil.
A sucrose time. This ancient myth,
man's evolution from sugar cane
—and reborning.

Here the agony,
twenty million brought from Africa.
Plantation's industry
Whiplash!

More sun and rain.
Fevered rhythms,
the longing to be free
one last time.

The buildings rise
higher in London.
Europe's walls
without ears.
Further whiplash, frenzy
of bones rattling
in wayward galleys.

Atlantic waters rising.
Foam of blood.
Wilberforce, Caxton.
Canning. The English parliament
now ready to lurch over.

Indentured, I listen on—
I am sucrose, too. Less flesh.
In the corners of the furrowed fields,
I breathe in the smell.
Saccharine—

This hour of sun, evolving
Once more. Land overturned.
Ground seething
with hands still on deck.
Backs welted,

groins sweating, the meeting
with you. Face to face
as we are grounded.

Lives

A beginning storm sets my blood racing—
I imagine the past with drum-beats—
Atavistic again
I am memory of the tropics
I listen to the hoof-beats
In the careering clouds.

I am watchful as always, meandering
with each spell of rain, each set-back
to the ground.

I wait my turn—
Stepping out with ritual.
I build canoes from the heat
Of my insides, skin bark—
Blood coursing round a cambium-heart

I am now Raleigh making up for lost time
I bend and turn through the winding thickets
My veins reek of silver and gold
I am at the Orinoco—

my eyes meet at the limit of ground and sky
I am history in the making
I am topsy-turvy once more.

Rehearsal

*"Language the chameleon seeks to explain
the chameleon reality." A.I.*

Old father tongue sticking out
over the fenced yard,
scampering out from the coop,
this reptilean self
breaking out without a warning—

changeable again, across the barrier
scattering feathers—
a life gone rampant
in dreams; the insane among us presenting
emblems from the scuttled sea—

all talk, old words, dropping scales
the dung of reality, moon-shape
pitching stars from the tips
of my fingers, blood oozing at the thighs
wetting the ground to form our roots

Posterity

As I am not
Pythagorean
everybody talks
a snake slithering
a ball rolls into
thick grass—
a grandfather whom I
hardly knew
about to have a stroke

A jolt and cry—
everyone rushes
grandmother's collapse next:
the sick among us
foreshadowing death

And amidst the sameness
of trees
a grandfather transmigrates
bird's song
in my ears—

being too young to remember
much else
I salve memory
growing up,
listening everywhere
to the music of the spheres—
wishing the familiar earth
to spin   everlastingly

Rhapsodies

an uncle tries his best
to break out in madness
an aunt reshapes her life
with three children and more

a mother carries in her womb
her thwarted desire
she stitches portions of her skin
with each new child being born

I am somewhere in the loud notes
throbbing in the old brain
I haunt the folds of night
insisting that all is not well

I collect discarded bones
I stop the gaps of my nightmare
I bang on the empty drums
      alone

Photo by Don Nguyen

Jessica Hagedorn

Jessica Hagedorn currently lives in New York City where she writes, performs in the theater, and leads her band, The Gangster Choir. Her first book, Dangerous Music *(Momo's Press) is now in its third printing. Her most recent book,* Pet Food & Tropical Apparitions, *also published by Momo's Press, is the recipient of an American Book Award for 1983.*

Motown / Smokey Robinson

hey girl, how long you been here?
did you come with yr daddy in 1959 on a second-class boat
cryin' all the while cuz you didn't want to leave the barrio
the girls back there who wore their hair loose
lotsa orange lipstick and movies on sundays
quiapo market in the morning, yr grandma chewin' red tobacco
roast pig? . . . yeah, and it tasted good . . .
hey girl, did you haveta live in stockton with yr daddy
and talk to old farmers who immigrated in 1941?
did yr daddy promise you to a fifty-eight-year-old bachelor
who stank of cigars . . . and did you
run away to san francisco / go to poly high / rat your hair /
hang around woolworth's / chinatown at three in the morning
to go to the cow palace and catch SMOKEY ROBINSON
cry and scream at his gold jacket
Dance every friday night in the mission / go steady with ruben?
(yr daddy can't stand it cuz he's a spik.)
and the sailors you dreamed of in manila with yellow hair
did they take you to the beach to ride the ferris wheel?
Life's never been so fine!
you and carmen harmonize "be my baby" by the ronettes
and 1965 you get laid at a party / carmen's house
and you get pregnant and ruben marries you
and you give up harmonizing . . .
hey girl, you sleep without dreams
and remember the barrios and how it's all the same:
manila / the mission / chinatown / east l.a. / harlem / fillmore st.
and you're gettin' kinda fat and smokey robinson's gettin' old

> **so take a good look at my face / you see my smile
> looks outta place / if you look closer / it's easy to trace /
> the tracks of my tears . . .**

but he still looks good!!!

> **i don't want to / but i need you / seems like i'm always /
> thinkin' of you / though you do me wrong now / my love is
> strong now / you really gotta hold on me . . .**

The Woman Who Thought
She Was More Than a Samba

the woman who thought
she was more than a samba
rode underground trains
dressed up for dancing,
as usual

never mind
that she looked good
succulent like peaches
tattoos on her skin
enough to make
most men sigh

rats
strung out on methadone
rode underground trains
with her,
rats in a trance
scratching
balancing oblivious children
on their laps

rats in a trance
scratching
asleep
ears glued
to radios blaring
city music
metallic abrasive
hard city music

the woman who thought
she was more than a samba
rode underground trains
terrified
she'd forget
how to dance

her dreams
were filled with ghosts
young men she knew
who danced
with each other
consumed by
ambiguous dilemmas

grinding their narrow hips
to snakelike city music
metallic abrasive hard city music
grinding their narrow hips
against her sloping,

naked back
like buffalos
shedding their fur
against a tree
whispering—"it's a shame
you aren't a man ...
you have so much man
in you"

in brazil
the women samba
only with their legs
their faces are somber
and their upper torsos
never move

in haiti
people draw themselves
without arms
and don't seem
to dance at all

exuding matinee idol ambience
the young men she knew
wore white
and sported moustaches
"we are a tropical people"
they reminded her,
"the most innovative
in the universe"
they gyrated desperately
and stayed drunk in bars
"we're **in**, this year"

it's a shame
i weren't a man
and who's the woman here?
she often asked herself
sometimes she screamed:
i'm older than you think
i'm getting so sick of you
i can't even remember your names
you all look the same ...

she fell in love once
and the wounds never healed
it was romance
old as the hills
predictable in its maze
what medieval tapestry he wove
to keep her still

gazelles loped
past their window
and veils kept out the sun

she had her own take on things,
her perfume-scented version
of the story
never mind that
he always won,
leaving unfinished poems
under her bed
orchestras strung upside-down
from the ceiling
traces of blood as souvenirs
of their exclusive
combat zone

the woman who thought
she was more than a samba
carried her solitude around
in pouches made of chinese silk
changing her jewelry
with each new lover
insisting they move
with sullen grace
stressing the importance
of style
on a dance floor
how arrogantly they might
hold up
their leonine heads

her dreams were filled with ghosts
perched on her bony wrists
grinning gargoyles
who menaced her every step
and wouldn't
let her go

she longed to be
her mother
in a silver dress
some softly fading memory
lifting her legs
in a sinuous tango

Ming The Merciless

> dancing on the edge / of a razor blade
> ming / king of the lionmen
> sing / bring us to the planet
> of no return ...

king of the lionmen
come dancing in my tube
sing, ming, sing ...
blink sloe-eyed phantasy
and touch me where
there's always hot water
in this house

o flying angel
o pteradactyl
your rocket glides
like a bullet

you are the asian nightmare
the yellow peril
the domino theory
the current fashion trend

ming, merciless ming
come dancing in my tube
the silver edges of your cloak
slice through my skin
and king vulgar's cardboard wings
flap-flap in death
(for you)

o ming, merciless ming,
the silver edges of your cloak
cut hearts in two
the blood red dimensions
that trace american galaxies

you are the asian nightmare
the yellow peril
the domino theory
the current fashion trend

sing, ming, sing ...
whistle the final notes
of your serialized abuse
cinema life
cinema death
cinema of ethnic prurient interest

o flying angel
o pteradactyl
your rocket glides
like a bullet
and touches me where
there's always hot water
in this house

Song for my Father

i arrive
in the unbearable heat
the sun's stillness
stretching across
the land's silence
people staring out
from airport cages
thousands of miles
later
and i have not yet understood
my obsession to return

and twelve years
is fast
inside my brain
exploding like tears

i could show you
but you already know.

you greet me
and i see
it is you
you all the time
pulling me back
towards this space

letters are the memory
i carry with me
the unspoken name
of you,
my father

in new york
they ask me if i'm puerto rican
and do i live in queens?

i listen to pop stations
chant to iemaja
convinced i'm really brazilian
and you a riverboat gambler
shooting dice in macao
during the war

roaches fly around us
like bats in twilight
and barry white grunts
in fashionable discotheques
setting the pace
for guerillas to grind

the president's wife
has a fondness for concert pianists
and gossip is integral
to conversation

if you eat enough papaya
your sex drive diminishes
lorenza paints my nails blue
and we giggle at the dinner table
aunts and whores
brothers and homosexuals
a contessa with chinese eyes
and an uncle cranky with loneliness
he carries an american passport
like me

and here we are,
cathedrals in our thighs
banana trees for breasts
and history all mixed up
saxophones in our voices
when we scream
the love of rhythms
inherent
when we dance

they can latin here
and shoot you
for the wrong glance
eyes that kill
eyes that kill

dope dealers are executed
in public
and senators go mad
in prison camps
the nightclubs are burning
with indifference
curfew drawing near
soldiers lurk in jeeps
of dawn warzones
as the president's daughter
boogies nostalgically
under the gaze
of sixteen smooth bodyguards
and decay is forever
even in the rage
of humorless revolutionaries

in hotel lobbies
we drink rum
testing each other's wit

snakes sometimes crawl
in our beds
but what can you do
in the heat
the laziness makes you love
so easily

you smile like buddha
from madrid
urging me to swim with you
the water is clear
with corpses
of dragonflies and
mosquitoes

i'm writing different poems now
my dreams have become reptilian
and green

everything green, green
and hot

eyes that kill
eyes that kill

women slither
in and out of barroom doorways
their tongues massage
the terror from your nightmares
the lizard hissing nervously
as he watches
you breathe

i am trapped
by overripe mangoes
i am trapped
by the beautiful sadness of women
i am trapped
by priests and nuns
whispering my name
in confession boxes
i am trapped
by antiques and the music
of the future

and leaving you
again and again
for america,
the loneliest of countries

my words change ...
sometimes
i even forget english.

Kimiko Hahn

The gut is essential. It informs what the mind edits, what the heart cultivates, what the spirit acts out. As far as subject matter my Japanese American background often rises especially from my mother's birthplace, Maui. Though I only visited my grandparents a few times each time penetrated my memory and sense of identity. But I write about whatever moves me—from nuclear disarmament issues to love. Having recently studied Japanese one of my main influences now is Kawabata Yasunari. I would like to write poetry the way he composed prose. And I believe, as others, that a more "self conscious" interest in structure (is there such a thing as "free" verse) is approaching; but we can't go backward so it won't be strictly stuff like iambic pentameter. We will use what free verse has allowed us to explore. For me that means half-rhyme and double meanings in particular. A new structure. Choices for change. This is true of my personal life and politics.

Kimiko Hahn is on the Editorial Board of Bridge: Asian American Perspectives *and on the Executive Committee of the American Writers Congress. She organized and moderated a panel of Asian American writers at the American Writers Congress in October, 1981.*

When You Leave

This sadness could only be a color
if we call it *momoiro*, Japanese

for *peach-color*, as in the first story
mother told us: It is the color of the hero's skin

when the barren woman discovered him
inside a peach floating down the river.

And of the banner and gloves she sewed
when he left her to battle the horsemen, then found himself

torn, like fruit off a tree. Even when he met a monkey,
dog and bird he could not release

the color he saw when he closed his eyes. In his boat
the lap of the waves against the hold

was too intimate as he leaned back to sleep. He wanted
to leave all thoughts of peach behind him —

the fruit that brought him to her
and she, the one who opened the color forever.

Daughter

Although I'm oldest I can't
be the one who paints

or speaks grandmother's language
like a picture-bride marriage

to a still life: a plate
of oranges, plums and grapes

one takes care to arrange
precise as syntax — as a passage

one must translate
for someone else. That

is the greater danger
than waking with a stranger.

Dance Instructions for a Young Girl

Stand: knees slightly
bent, toes in *posed*
you watch the hawk over the river
curve, until his voice, shoulders back
gently *overcome by Seiji's mouth*
against yours, the white breath, and elbows
close to your side. *The silk cords*
and sash crush your lungs you are
young — beautiful, and almost
elegant. The layers of cloth pastel,
bright red, and moist
twist around. Follow his flow
of steps, a shallow stream between rocks
the carp. Seiji draws your hand
toward him or a stroke.
Before you look back turn your chin
in a figure eight, tilt, balance
then kneel quickly *the relief of cloth*
pulled off. Bow to him and the audience.
When you straighten, his black and red lines
against the white powder
are drawn, as his gesture
and step, perfectly. More perfectly *the weight*
of his chest than your own, although his
belong to you, a woman.

Note: Geisha were often told to imitate the female impersonator Kabuki actors.

A Girl Combs Her Hair

Recently cut she is unaccustomed
to the blunt end

just above her moist shoulders.
Even in the morning

the air feels close — closer
than his shirt

slipped over her head.
The comb glides through the luster,

and stops short.
She thinks of fingers. Hands

gripping the small of her back. She leans
against the wall. He could have

brought flowers. The girl wants
to sit for a while on the fire escape:

to listen to the water
draining the open fire hydrant

and cooling the street and children —
to figure out the look he gave

when she turned and small hairs
scattered across the pillow. But already

it's so oppressive. She would collect
all her combs and snap them in half

but a scent keeps her
from moving from the sheets.

By her sandals she notices an orchid
in white tissue. She reaches.

Dianne Hai-Jew

Second generation Chinese, Diane was born the second daughter (of three) of Harold and Amy Sheung Jew in Huntsville, Alabama. Having received over thirty awards, she entered the University of Washington at 15 through the UW Early Entrance Program, and will graduate in 1984 with a B.A. in psychology and another in English.

On campus, she is starting her second year as the English editor for the Chinese Student Association Tung Fung *magazine. She has worked as a volunteer phoneworker for the Seattle Crisis Clinic, and is a three-year March of Dimes Walk-America participant.*

Her poems have appeared or are forthcoming in: Matrix, Creative Sources, Bricolage, Orphic Lute, Spindrift, Poetry Seattle, Tung Fung, *and others.*

She attends local plays, poetry readings, art shows, garage sales, concerts, and frequents coffee shops with friends in her spare time. A practiced procrastinator, Diane has read magazines, novels, poetry, short stories, or written fiction—on twelve hour sprees on occasion.

Foreign Soil, Days Ago, *and* Thirst of the Dragon *were written for her maternal grandparents: Gim and Hor Chun Jueng.*

Days Ago

Like a crumpled paper cutout,
a body is outlined
through sterilized hospital
sheets stretched over a cold
slab of bed. Fluorescent
overheads whitewash
the walls and pencil-detail
shadows on the woman's half-
turned face. The spicy
aftertaste of Hong Kong
incense lingers. On the window
sill shelving, dentures float
in a plastic cup of yellow
fluid, set atop the woman's
large scrapbook, flapping
with feathery clippings, now
as fine as toilet paper.
A chess set waits in a one-step
checkmate, left by visitors
months ago. In the walk-in
closet, dresses cling sparsely
on the metal rail; the chiffons,
fitted to the measurements
of a wasted body, have since
been stolen—marked by empty
hangers. Held in the splinter
between dreams and waking,
her skin stretched hand
maneuvers through the sprays
of washed out perm fanned
on the stark foam pillows.
She mumbles, sound of sleep
and hollow air from her puckered
mouth. Brown eyes overcast
with translucent splotches of
blue membrane focus on the 1979
calendar—nurse's handwriting
reminding her of the daughter
who should have arrived
for a visit days ago.

Thirst of the Dragon

Sharp air folds like giftwrap
and queue-braids water on rocks.
Ribs pressed on the ship rail,
I listen to your tattered
voice crumple, lifting
and snapping like sails;
you ask if I'd noticed
how the push and pull of waves
imitate hands kneading hombough
dough.

We balance on water-washed
decks and throw laughter
out like red New Year's streamers.
You say all ships remind you
of the freighter that juggled
you from Hong Kong to Canada
to the States: waves sucking foam
at the bow, breath of steam, sting
of salt.

Your black-gold jacket
fits tight on the shoulder
like a harness and rides to the waist,
but you say it's a ship voyage
tradition. You tell me that
you're a sojourner, but the hands
that once opened to welcome
you back are held akimbo.

Foreign sounds, unborn
in your hollow pronunciations
speak in your receding eyes
and I hold your 73-year
worn body to mine, trying
to anchor you to a way alien,
while I watch you sink
like an ocean-emptied
bottle, trying to collect a rich
wine vintage—long diluted.

This Night

for Jim W. Yamasaki

Taste of peaked champagne
dry like salt in my throat,
I twist in your hands
and watch the string
of Japanese tissue roses
unfold, a fist of the Issei.
From the open shutters,
pine rustles like broom straw.
We lie still to listen.

In the newborn calm
after a Midwest rainstorm,
when wind-weary cones drop
back on hard soil,
we have fallen.
Air spills like rain over us;
the moment for dreams passes,
untallied. Words pelt heavy
and dissolve into this night
as sumi strokes to wet rice
paper sheaths. We huddle
like children saving warmth.

High tide stealing sand
from under our feet,
we pull closer. But the end
was written before we turned
page one, lines scribed
on open palms. I recall
your laughter, your voice,
until the silence
becomes a noise.
You roll away.

Foreign Soil

Visiting Grandpa years ago, I
remember the tender tree he'd
planted as a boy in America, a seed
pocket-saved before the stormy
ship ride to the States. The tree
stretched so high, I thought it tugged
at clouds rumbing by, bursting
them like a pin to a balloon,
releasing floodgates of rain, needles
of sleet, so unlike the warm,
smooth Wunsind river water. Clawing
the trunk, heels feeling for a notch,
I reached for the first branch.

Six years later, climbing on lower
boughs in faded denim overalls, rubber-
banded pigtails, a fresh shoestring
of licorice clenched between a front
row of permanent teeth, I'd look
down and wonder if I dared to jump—
but looking up, the ground seemed
closer. Watching Grandpa stroke
the coarse bark, prune branches like
layering a French haircut and picking
hard, bitter fruit to ripen, days spent
on window sills basking in a cold
sun, I would stand hugging the trunk.
My fingers never met.

Hair feathered back in crooked steps,
teeth harnessed in braces, I'd talk
politics, school and family gossip
whenever we visited St. Louis. Late nights
after six-course dinners, I would tiptoe
out to feel the dewy crisp of leaves,
weigh fruit in the palm of my hand,
bobbing the branches. I thought I saw
a shadowed face watch me from Grandpa's
room while I tried to climb thick
branches with etiquette, riding
the heavy wood like a lady, legs
swung over to one side.

Sounds of graduation parties still
clear, I visit—this time, alone. I see
this "heen jun thloot le" tree
stops long before the sky even begins.
The crusted trunk, drained and weighted
with fungi, marred by Midwest ice
winters, is hollowed and splintered
like salt driftwood. Grandpa says
he is too tired to mother the China
tree, too tired to raise himself upon his
elbows to look. Now I know this fisted tree
can no longer hold my weight.

Gail N. Harada

Gail N. Harada was born in Honolulu, Hawaii and spent part of her childhood in Japan. She attended the University of Hawaii, earned an A.B. in English from Stanford University, and has an M.F.A. in English from the University of Iowa. She is currently working for a television station and teaching sporadically in the Poets-In-The-Schools program. Her poems have appeared in Wahine O Hawaii *(a special issue of Seaweeds & Constructions),* Bamboo Ridge: The Hawaii Writers' Quarterly, Hawaii Review, *and* Talk Story: An Anthology of Hawaii's Local Writers. *Her poem "Painted Passages" has been produced into a videotape as part of a collaboration with filmmaker Robert Pennybacker and artist Noe Tanigawa.*

First Winter

We are far from what held us then.
You will not live again in that house
where you could hear footsteps
shuffling through the long ironwood needles,
and there are houses to which I will not return.

Now you send letters about your new life,
but sometimes there is that reflection back.
You write "The spy life is over"
we are young girls no longer.
The language you are learning
is melodious and quick.
You say you are beginning to dream in it.
You tell me of islands lovelier than any vision,
and of three bays:
Anse Vata, Baie des Citrons, Baie de l'Orphelinat.

I will tell you of the river at night
and what it is to want to walk closer to its edge.
I will tell you of the snow which turns one back
into the curve of the body,
that quiet and its steady falling
which keeps me by the window for hours,
of a silence those ironwoods
never gave, not even after a light rain.

New Year

This is the old way,
the whole clan gathered,
the rice steaming over the charcoal,
the women in the room, talking,
a layer of potato starch on the table.

This is the old way,
the father watching his son lift the mallet,
pound the rice, pound mochi,
the children watching or playing,
the run of the dough to the women,
the rolling of the round cakes.

This is the old way,
eating ozoni, new year's soup:
mochi for longevity,
daikon, long white radish
rooted firmly like families;
eating burdock, also deeply rooted,
fish for general good luck,
and lotus root, wheel of life.

This is the old way,
setting off firecrackers
to drive away evil spirits,
leaving the driveways red for good fortune.

The new year arrives,
deaf, smelling of gunpowder.

Pomegranate

Even now she sometimes
thinks of the child
she might have had.
The woman had been kind,
chanting Hawaiian over the boiled pomegranates
night after night.
The hot brew stank,
made the girl nauseous.
The boiled fruit were soft,
brown, bitter.
Later, curious, she tried a fresh pomegranate.
She sliced through the leathery skin
to the chambers of red seeds,
each seed a jewel, a fish egg
tipped with blood.
She ate it deliberately,
pulling seed from skin,
staining her fingers with the sweet juice.

Painted Passages

I.

The even weave of the canvas
becomes as familiar
as childhood, perhaps,
an expanse of sky or sea,
the ground we walk on barefoot,
and the task at hand seems clear.
It is what we wish for,
secretly,
like a craving for tamarinds
or shave ice,
or the taste of salt
water.
It is a beginning.
Rain.
A spring that flows
into a pond,
a stream,
the sea.
The frame must be perfectly
true.
Push its corners into a door.
Measure it with steel tape.
Stretch the canvas over the frame
and the instinct of experience
takes over.
Pull the canvas.
Feel the taut
surface
tight and even.
A drum to beat out soundless rhythm.
Prepare the canvas to receive color.
Size it with something supple enough,
rabbit or calfskin glue.
Prime it
with an unbelievable whiteness—
No-snow, no-cloud, no color.
This is the whiteness of light,
of sleep,
of the space behind human eyes.
This is the rhythm of labor,
of sweat.
The hands and fingertips remember its feel
like a prodigal remembers a house,
a room,
the given colors of a landscape.

II.

Your mother wants you
to come home,
and keeps telling me so,
believing in the persuasive powers
of friendship.
She's afraid for you,
living on the edge
in what she thinks is the crime capital
of the universe,
where, according to Charles Osgood,
dog bites are down
and human bites are up 23% this year.

But your letters are filled only
with the excitement of living
in a city that never sleeps,
and with the heady whirl
of art openings, galleries,
and the most incredible people—
people who remind one not so much of jewels,
as they do of brilliant neon lights
that stun you with their electricity.

Come back to New York and be famous,
you tell me.
Opportunity is just waiting to be picked
like a ripe purple plum
in the Big Apple, you say,
trying to persuade me
across an entire ocean and continent
again.
And sometimes those bright lights you thrive on
almost feel like the sun
to me.   Almost.

What can I say to explain this
or any other choice?
When I was on the mainland,
the torpor of winter
kept depositing itself
on my tropic bones,
making me long
for the blue Pacific Ocean,
the ripeness of mangoes,
the crests of waves in moonlight,
the unforgettable greens of the Koolaus,
and this island that shudders
under the growing weight of its concrete,
waiting.

I try to shape all these colors,
define or obliterate them
with black or white.
What pulls me here is not nostalgia,
but a conviction
deeper than blood.

III.

Just a few strokes
of inspiration,
a little light
to fly towards,
is all I ask.

What consumes me
is rain in the morning,
the daily bowl of rice,
the small everyday tasks,
and some passage
to another side
of home.

Garrett Kaoru Hongo

Garrett Kaoru Hongo was born in the Territory of Hawaii near what is now Hawaii Volcanoes National Park. He grew up in Gardena, California and was educated at Pomona College, The University of Michigan, and the University of California at Irvine where he earned his M.F.A. in English. His poetry has appeared in The New Yorker, Antaeus, The Nation, Poetry Northwest, *and the* Honolulu Star-Bulletin.* *He has received the Thomas J. Watson Fellowship, the Hopwood Prize,* The Nation/Discovery Award, *and the NEA Fellowship. He has taught at the University of Washington, the University of Southern California, and UC Irvine where this coming year he will be teaching the graduate workshop.* Yellow Light, *his first book of poems, was published by Wesleyan University Press in 1982.*

Poetry is a craft, a faith, and, for the most part, a real privilege. It is also a tool of liberation and an instrument of oppression. As there are bad teachers and politicians, so are there bad poets, false poets, and poseurs. The title is always open for the taking—which is both the trouble and the terrible beauty of it—with the best of us refusing but always seeming to defend it. Irony, wit, ethnic nationalism, and other ideologies have all had their fads and poetry has suffered them all. For me, poetry has been a way towards self-definition and the engagement of an imagined community. More and more though, I'd like it to become a way of mystery and syncretic metaphysics, beautiful to write, read, and hear spoken aloud without ignoring the terror and confusions of our time.

Re lyric poetry—What it is—a fiction that imitates, hopefully with grace, the construction of a consciousness, say in apprehension of a particular scene or in contemplation of an object or a problem (philosophical, mathematical, aesthetic, literary—it doesn't matter). The Chinese poets started out with landscapes, describing a scene and using it to summon up some pronouncement about their own lives, the political situation, or the foolishness of learning. It was a brave and religious sort of poetry, a kind of divination actually, trusting the poem to perform as a kind of oracle for the spirit world, a gateway into higher, perhaps redeemed consciousness. Poetry was only one of the things that did this—tortoise shells, yarrow stalks, burnt oracle bones, tarnished coins, crazy hermaphroditic mediums,

and paper fortunes drawn from an earthenware jar in the village market-
place all performed similar if more portentous or trivial functions. We don't
do this too much in American culture, dominated as we are by suburban
and falsely pastoral values. Maybe we follow a baseball team (I myself love
the Dodgers and can't help it) and study the spring predictions in Sports
Illustrated, buy handicap sheets for the horse races, read horoscopes or else
Wall Street tip-sheets depending. We compare notes, press opinions, argue
a little, but pretty much keep our worries about self and fortune fairly
private.

   Somewhat like the blues, however, poetry provides a stylized but often
eloquent way to speak one's worried mind and even offer up a question or
two to higher powers about one's fate. Most of the time the asking's enough
(relief is just a sonnet away), though once in a while we're surprised and
shaken by a mysterious response.

*He was founding director of the Asian Exclusion Act, a Seattle-based
theater group, and Co-Coordinator of the Pacific Northwest Asian Ameri-
can Writers Conference. With Alan Lau and Lawson Inada, he wrote THE
BUDDHA BANDITS DOWN HIGHWAY 99.

Hiking Up Hieizan with Alam Lau/
Buddha's Birthday 1974

It's a long hot walk up Fathead Mountain you know
is that
what you call it sure he said Fathead Mountain
Hieizan's
too hard to say and it looks like a big fat head
the Buddha
at Todaiji you know but shit let's get started man
what you
bring for lunch Hongo *nigiri* and *umeboshi* inside
or did you
go meat today bring you some ham sandwich kinda
jive
no I said it's just *musubi* with sesame seeds
and beef
teriyaki and *takuan* man you know the old *pikniku*
no niku
like at *kenjinkai* and *Foru Jurai* as Lawson says
yeah
where's he at now Ashland doing his thing making us
a visible minority
I'd sure like to meet him someday you will I said
well let's
hit it and head up into the *susuki* and *yamazakura* trees
buddy
this mountain ain't gonna get no lower you know

STARTED UP THE TRAIL

huffing and puffing the chuff and fluff of Japanese
dandelions
fuzzy balloons banging into us drifting downwind down
the trail
floating with the cold air sinking down the mountain
towards town
the ricefields and farmshacks below us two Buddha
Bandits
chugging uphill over there in the *sasa* and bamboo
bramble
the first time I ever heard an *uguisu* sounds like
a goddamn
flutophone or something man you ever see one up close
Alan
no he said only in paintings and stuff it's hard
to get
next to one of those more skittish than Japanese
virgins
don't want your ass anywhere near them yeah
I know
I said busting up they want themselves a
whiteboy
filthy Orange County rich with a Porsche and
IBM stocks
not no raggedyass Buddhahead *Botan Ame* junkie
man and
for damn sure not no Chonk chump sucker
I know
what you mean it's the tourist girls you
gotta get
man over at the Stardust or Frisco Disco on
Kawaramachi
man they're all there tall and long-legged
and looking
for business Alan said oh yeah I said no shit
damn it's
dusty pass me the canteen

CUTTING UP THROUGH CEDAR

trees there's some snorting and scuffling in
the bushes
up ahead must be a wild pig digging for
potatoes
do they attack people I said no he said only
punks from
Gardena think they cool fuck you Lau can't
wait till
we get a view you can see all the temples the
tile roofs
with tv antennas sticking up in the haze
how bout

72

the Takanogawa yeah it's still clear before
it runs
into the Kamo you can see the sandbars and
patches of
waterweeds no shit *ukigusa* it's called how
come you
know so much and still can't speak the lingo
too good
you been here over three years Lau
I know
enough to buy *miso* and *tofu* take a bath
argue with
my landlord and even make a pass if
I want
you're too hip I said stepping up the

STEPSTONES

some unknown Buddhist trailcrew a thousand
years ago
musta done it carved it right into the damn
fucking
mountain yeah they'll carve a piece of sutra
right into
the granite sometimes no shit look there's
a *jizo*
up there were the trail bends got a bib
on it see
a bib what they do that for anyway man
for good
luck to make your kids grow up smart
fool if
your folks had done it for you
you wouldn't
be so damned ignorant it's smooth granite
shaped like
a half-pint snowman big head eyes nose
and mouth
just scratched on eyes heavy-lidded as if in meditation
just a small Enin smile I know something
you don't
rub the shining stomach for good luck
get a
flat rock and balance it on his head
a graduation
cap aura of wisdom let's go Hongo there's
lots more
up the trail you can read me the sutras in
his back
on the way down don't they ever scratch
a KILROY
WAS HERE or you know TAROKAJA LOVES
SACHIKO

or something I ask no not on the
jizo man
they do it on walls and big rocks and
stuff you
know draw an umbrella and put their names
under it
side by side *aikasa* love umbrella they
call it

HEY MAN

some boy scouts no a *karate* club up ahead
they are
kicking ass up this trail some bunch of
macho Mishimas
look at them they got rucksacks fulla rocks
on their backs
crazyass fuckers running up the trail yet
what they tryna
prove they got rotary power with fuel injected
shoyu or something
just working out man they probably got a
sake party
waiting for them at the top what we got
just a
view and cup of tea at the temple man
ain't that
enough depends on if you're a felonious
monk on the
lam or a Buddhahead tryna work a scam
I said
how are you keeping yourself alive anyway Alan
teach English
at UNESCO over on Horikawa oh yeah you
get enough
oh sure plenty I got me a 6' x 12' three
mat room
rice every day *miso* soup green onions
cabbage spinach
tofu pumpkins and sweet black beans once
a week don't
you eat any meat Alan no *kawai so ni* no
sentient beings
man not even no fish or eggs or cheese
or nuthin
I eat cheese and lots of ice cream when
I can get
it you tryna buck for Buddha Second Class
I said
no just don't wanna give nobody no pain
man but shit
not even no fish or *saba* or *sashimi* or squid
satojoyu

steamed rock cod clams in black bean sauce
man you
turning your back on your heritage selling
your soulfood
short man I said yeah he said but tryna save
my soul
no shit man no shit I said no shit no shit he said
no shit

GRABBING HOLD OF A TREE LIMB

stepping out on the rock ledge pointing
look Garrett
the hawks slow pinwheels circling over
rice paddies
green as Oregon fanning out like a
royal flush
the songs of fieldworkers Japanese *campesinos*
carrying up
the mountain the two of us leaning into the wind
straining to hear
beanplants and sunflowers in California stretching
toward the sun

LET'S BREAK FOR LUNCH

get into some good *gohan* some Gardena
grease boy
I sure miss *jalapena* with my *teriyaki*
you know
any songs or poems by heart man you know
the usual
and so Alan recites some T'ao Ch'ien
for starters
an old man weeding his garden knocking dirt
off the *daikon*
singing songs of geese in the wind mallards
cruising the
Yellow River just bitchin I do one from Hawaii
my grandfather
taught me rain and waterfalls plumeria the
usual and try
some of this *manju* man it's sweet goes good
after all that
salty stuff you want a *mikan* man and so we
share a couple
mandarins they're called back home tiny as
transistor radios

BACK HOME

back home my folks work and watch tv worry about
gas prices
the 5 a.m. lineups at Kozai's Texaco back home

they send
me clippings from the sports page the *Holiday
Rafu*
my brother's gigging in Vegas tryna make it
back home
back home Cynthia's shelving books filing records
writes me
I love you I love you *querida mia* I love you
back home
they all work so damn hard get two weeks off
for good
behavior my folks go to Yosemite in a Winnebago
back home
why didn't they ever teach me about the
Buddha
why didn't I learn to love them more why
am I here
On Hieizan eating rice singing songs in
Hawaiian and
Japanese why do the geese cry and mountains
slouch toward
the sea why does the sky pour fire by midday
why are
there so many of us who've forgotten what it
means to praise the earth and those we love?

4;xi;78

Patricia Y. Ikeda

It's so important for poets to wake up and say, "Look at the trees!" and "It was just like this. . ." Our lives and our poetry aren't separate. I believe in kinship and nature as two inexhaustible sources. What else is there? I've been in various parts of the Midwest for 29 years, have degrees from Oberlin College and the University of Iowa, and right now am in Michigan, working as office manager for the Michigan Abortion Rights Action League. I have been studying t'ai chi and sitting with friends at the Zen Buddhist Temple of Ann Arbor for about a year now. So I can really see that strong peacefulness and harmony, especially in these Asian traditions, are important to my present way of life. I've had to discover them for myself, of course, and to realize that, as a Japanese-American, my being neither Japanese nor mainstream white American gives me a great deal of freedom. And freedom, like peace, isn't passive. I'm grappling with my poetry these days, asking "What is a poem?" Again.

Prior publications:

Book of poetry: House of Wood, House of Salt, *Cleveland State University Press, 1978. Cleveland, Ohio.*

Poems published in Poetry Northwest, Field, Epoch, Pocket Pal.

A Card Game: Kinjiro Sawada

1.

We sit in the basement kitchen, arranging
hana-fuda cards in suites. He's dressed, as always,
in stale blue pajamas. Dead for a decade,
we don't mind. Just one more language
between us. The small stiff cards fan: one year.
Pine, plum, cherry, paulownia, maple.
The words I know are *ume* and *sakura*.
Both in blossom.

2.

He came from samurai and silk farmers.
He shipped to Hawaii.
He rode a roan horse through Libby's red fields.
He married a girl who cleaned officers' quarters.
He bought a dry-goods store on Cane Street.
He prayed and wrote poetry.
When government agents searched the house
he surrendered his pen-knife.
I met him twice.

3.

The birthday party: his seventieth year
by Japanese count, 69 + 1 in the womb.
He told me I was born in Year of the Horse
but the good, not the ominous horse.
Still, I know no Japanese would marry me.
I'm supposed to be stubborn. I am.
I remember how he sat, hieratic,
weighed down by the lei of silver dollars
won by my Vegas-hopping aunts and uncles.
One more year. The cards are shuffled,
the red-headed stork, the deer,
the empty field with no moon.

4.

Our tie is formal. First grandchild
and old man, we sit on the floor.
His house smells like incense and mold.
He teaches me the name he gave me,
brushing *Yo-shi-ko* in thick black strokes.
Ten years. Over my desk
I've hung the Buddhist prayer he copied,
the Hannyashingyo, its flickering, difficult
characters only a priest can read.

Recovery

1.

Maybe this is what *ghost* is: one
who left hardly a trace,
like the uncle driving the tractor home
in Indiana, his face flaring once
in the drunk man's headlights
and after the yell of crushed metal
the cicadas starting up, the moist drift
of growing corn from the black fields.

2.

When the afternoon holds
its breath and starlings
hunch in the trees,
what do I wait for?
There are secrets
in the wine-dark underleaves
of the copper beech, and all day
I've felt like the spark
of a struck flint, the flame.

3.

Black locust, ailanthus,
birch: another October
weaves into weaker light,
and beneath our feet
the earth gives up
its charred spice.

Old friend, uncle,
where are you leading me now?

Your voice, less familiar,
sounds down the rattling path,
and I try to step
more quietly, as if
entering a farm house at night,
sensing my way by the stilled air
around the worn furniture.

I try to follow
as I lie down, each breath
the interval between
these down-drifting leaves.

4.

The gray transformers
on the alley's wooden scaffold
hunch and grow more dense. At this hour
I no longer hear the nighthawks'
scraping cries, and the sky
grows grainy and mindless.

I have sat up all night, convinced
that something is being asked
to be recovered, that somewhere
an old doorway in the earth is opening,
releasing what I've lost. And yet
as I reach forward to turn off the lamp
and the room fills with quiet fire
and pigeons scuffle on the window sill,
I don't know. I don't know.

Translations

I. Hibiscus

In the basement my mother tended
her shelves of potted plants, beneath
the blue-white flicker of fluorescent lights.
Through the hard Ohio winters, when
grain froze in the bird feeder, when
snow drifted in stiff waves against the door,
she raised her small jungle and lived there;
looking back, I think I understand
more fully now her happiness
when the hibiscus opened its one-day bloom.

That was her way of going home
where hibiscus fountained from bushes
on pathways leading to the baseball field
behind Cane Street's row of dingy stores,
their windows smeared with the red dust
of Hawaii's clay soil, the yards littered
with avocados that fell and blackened.
I remember their soapy, rotting smell
mingling with the mosquito repellent
burned in brittle green coils.

But what happened there I must guess
or imagine — sunlight flaring
from the red circle of the Rising Sun
revealed as the planes banked, heading
for Pearl Harbor while children yelled
attack! attack! and my grandfather,
his head bent beneath the store's small lamp,
looked up from a tray of dismantled watches,
the tiny screwdriver poised in his hand ...

II. Snake

Look, says my mother, opening the scroll,
one stroke of the brush!
A headless snake uncoils beneath her hands,
its black body as strong
and ungraspable as a river.
What skill could pull the inky brush
across the page, surely as a shout
straight from the belly?

Smoothing the insect-rusted paper,
red tiger and lotus seals, I hold
what remains of the day in Japan
when the priest bent over, and placed
an ink-blot on the gill-like darkness
where the snake's head should be.
He might have said: *See how it winds*

into uncertainty, the present
you see less clearly than the past,
and this, you have yet to live.
Or maybe nothing was said before
he blew gently, and the ink sprayed
in a thin arc that feathered at its end,
the possibilities of my grandfather's life
opening into the white page.

I've hung the snake above my bed.
At night, when I study it
in the half-light of my city room,
it rises like smoke.

III.　　Fire

The letter from Tokyo says:
Our third snowfall. Snow falling,
like plum blossoms, means change.
My second cousin in Fukushima,
a woman I did not know existed,
burned herself and her house to the ground.
The thin blue paper is stamped with a crane,
its wings unfurling.

If each moment consumes itself
completely before yielding the next,
then what can I know of history?
Maybe the past is a paper house
and in separate rooms a woman is bending
to touch a flower's crinkled red lip,
another woman is rattling a box of matches,
and a man who has snapped the back
of a mended watch in place leans back,
rubs his eyes, sighs, turns off
the lamp and goes home.

I want to stand beside them
and demand the old stories,
ones that start with "once upon a time,"
and stories of burning and betrayal.
I want them to answer my fears.
But they're quiet now, intent on private
and completed tasks. I must go on
standing outside their lives,
inventing translations.

Photo by Christopher Briscoe

Lawson Fusao Inada

Lawson Inada is the author of BEFORE THE WAR, and an editor of AIIIEEEEE! Professor of English at Southern Oregon State College.

Since When As Ever More

I. Since

Since born. Since beginning. Since dawn.

Since you. Since it. Since since. Since on.

Since conception, since is, since found.

Since you were here anyway.
Since you came.
Since you went away.
Since you were gone.
Since you called.
Since the creation of creation.
Since cognition crawls from the eye.
Since sense. Since sky.

Since—oh, when was it?
Since the last time, perhaps.
Since the battle. Since goodbye.

Since waves, since wings. Since the matter.
Since wind. Since sings, since cries.
Since the forces at work. Since wonder.
Since light, since sound. Since thunder.
Since the very first time, since time.
Since substance, since earth.
Since magnitude, since memory.
Since recognition. Since lament.
Since sweet, since soft, since scent.
Since gain, since loss, since gain.
Since distance. Since then.

Since yes.
Since again.
Since when.

Since.

II. When

When the touch takes shape.
When the such in profile.
When the much is more than ever.

When there is no mistaking.
When there are no mistakes.

When the still, the gradual.
When the blend and grow.

When it is there.
When you are now.
When the slightest movement.

When the earth.

When light, when heat, when actual.
When clarity, when resolve.

When the passage of shine.
When the clouds, the sounds.
When the above below.
When the know.
When the know.

When the flow.
When the flow.
When the flow.

When the first firsts.
When it counts.
When the last lasts.

When, oh, the stars were always there.
When the moon before and after.
When the long.

When the gratitude, the laughter.

When the stirrings, the turns.
When the then.

When, oh when, oh when, oh when?

When?

III. As

As it was in the beginning.
As a request, as persuasion, as happening.
As what you say it is.

As in the first warm days of summer among valleys.
As ridges, as rivers, as the predominance of thirst.
As well as welcome.

As work, as hunger, as sustenance.
As simple as that.

As relation, as communication.
As means, as need, as affirmation.
As simple as that.

As difficult as freedom.

As self as self. As affiliation.
As beckoning, as attempting, as begging for help.
As anger, as condition. As desperation.

As quest, as question, as belief, as wisdom.
As working, as learning, as trying and trying.

As pleading, as denying.
As getting on with it. As survival.
As doing what can. As conviction.
As the most, the utmost, as the situation.

As doubt, as defeat.
As pain, as outrage.
As you were.

As you will.

As courage.

As ever.

As.

IV. Ever

Ever. Enter ever. Ever in the guise of never.
Ever, always hiding.
Ever, always showing.

Ever this, ever that.
Ever whenever.

Ever early, ever late.
Ever uninvited, for that matter.
Ever and ever and ever.

Ever setting up some sort of rules.
Ever playing around.
Ever on a run, a cycle.
Ever at the gate, off and on.

Ever wise.
Ever not knowing.
Ever saying all right.
Ever not caring.

Ever doing it anyway.
Ever and ever, over and over.

Ever in the sunlight.
Ever in the unlight.

Ever suffering, ever smiling, ever all at once.
Ever never there. Ever everywhere.

Ever every.
Ever none.

Ever many.
Ever one.

Ever only.
Ever lonely.
Ever over all at once.

Ever and ever and ever.

Ever more.

Ever.

V. More

More. Morning. More and more. And more.

More all over the mind, the horizon. And more.

More, even, than you can imagine.
More, even, than you. And you. And you. And you.
More—that much. And more.

More than ever. And then some more.

More than words can say. And then some.

More than words cannot say. And more. And more.

More than you will ever know. And then some.

More than less, and less than more. Moreover.

More, much more, than more. And then some.

More and more and more: since when as ever more!

More and more and more.

More and more.

More!

Jaime Jacinto

Sometime near the end of the Qing Dynasty, a young man (with queue still intact) left Fujian Province for greener pastures across the South China Sea to Luzon in the Northern Philippines where he married a woman whose mother had lost her maidenhood to a spanish friar. From that union (learned from juicy family gossip) and many many generations later, I was born, a November child who, with the rest of my family, continued the cycle and crossed another sea to San Francisco where I spent my childhood and adolescence discovering cultural gems like baseball, television and the Detroit Sound (The Temptations, Marvin & Tammy et al.).

More recently, I've been trying to solve some contradictions created by my travels to other places, & dabbling in academia while trying to glean some of that street corner wisdom. My poetry is an outlet for that energy. I am a graduate of U.C. Santa Cruz where I studied under William Everson and George Hitchcock. I am currently completing an M.A. in TEFL (teaching English as a foreign language) while trying to finish a first book of poems. To finance this, I have disguised myself as a janitor sweeping out the hallways of a building on San Francisco's waterfront. The women in my life—Camille and Alexis my daughters, and Victoria, my wife, make it all worthwhile.

: Reflections on the Death of a Parrot

(or: a eulogy for a Tarzan matinee)

By a window overlooking tv antennas and bakery
smokestacks, lost in the smells of bread and
pastry, my parrot would perch in its cage, gnawing
an old broom handle, slowly turning it into
toothpicks. His white cage no match for the imagi-
nary rain forests of Rousseau's eye. No songs come
from this caged bird. Only the squawk of domes-
ticity. Reacting to the routine, to banquets of
water and peanuts, sleeping and shitting, the
animal necessities that invoke no nirvana. This
bird-monk, his zazen, just perching, meditating
distances between wire and open space. Eventually,
his boredom became mine, his frustration given in
me, and this morning, with a slap to his head
from my bambood flute, he took the first blessings
of reincarnation. With a swift stroke, not pre-
meditated and mine alone, like a child spitting
into his reflection of river water, I raised
my flute, swung it as an imagined wind, snapping
hollow bones and sinew, ruffling jade colored
feathers and the tune on my lips. Struck and
quivering, his thick black tongue unable to play
tricks. No faking jungle cries, no dark vines
to hide in, not even the heavy steam of monsoon
rains. And screeching his last breath, he let the
pain reach him, take him and I watched feeling
the joy of guilt shudder through me, my blood,
as I placed the flute back to my lips and blew
a melody composed of his bones and feathers, my
reflection losing itself in the dark globes of
his eyes.

: The Fire Breather, Mexico City

Every afternoon
when the rush-hour traffic
rages its way home
and twilight
begins to swirl
into the neon of La Avenida,
he is there
standing on the corner.

As you sit in your car
cursing for
the green light
you barely notice
how he sips gasoline
from a tin can
holds it in his mouth
and stepping onto
the crosswalk,
raises a match
to his lips
where the burns
have entered
to sour his lungs,
until that one
well-timed breath
when he spits
and torches
gray sweeps of sky.

Hidden in a span
of red light
there are thirty seconds
of hope,
for coins left behind
on the asphalt,
even without
the unravelling of tents
or cards of the fortuneteller,
this boy like the fumes of
a lonesome mirage,
his movable circus
burning from streetlight
to streetlight.

: The Beads

Late at night
I hear her whispering
beneath a gray shawl
pacing the hallway
and revisiting old sorrows
hands folded clasping
a string of beads
her eldest daughter
brought from Europe,
blessed by a holy man
who wore a diamond
on his finger.
Oh how she dreamed of kissing it!

in the yard
the rooster
has chosen his mount
and cackles at the turning moon.

There were times
I would close my eyes
and hide in her house
wondering whose footsteps
echoed on the marble floor,
and why the walls exhaled
the scent of funeral flowers.

In the hollow palm
of this darkness
Grandmother answers
with a lullaby,
for the son torn
by a flash of smoke
in the last war.
It is for him she sings
clothed in the dead silk
of her shawl
as her fingers
trace the cool beads
forever mourning themselves
into dust.

: Looking for Buddha

1   where to begin

warm stones gather the rainfall
speaking a gray language
i've tried to imitate.
i read books compiled
from anonymous scrolls,
i eat their dust
hoping to trace
the steps to heaven.
i toss bronze coins
deciphering oracles
of jade and brocaded silk.

Buddha
are you the drunk laughing at the moon?
are you the bitch-serpent coiling at her egg's release?
are you the wind pausing above the reeds?

2   old teachers

grandmother's lips move
as paper offerings
turn to ash.
old woman!
the years of childbearing
have left you mute
but tireless.
how can i answer to customs
and filial tradition?
the certainty of your years
makes you tremble,
remembering a childhood
of prayers and rain.

3   going back

when i was a child
i played with fireflies
tying thread to their legs
watching their light
dangle and glow
through mosquito nets
and evening would come
when we ambushed lizards,
their throats
their soft bellies
transparent and billowing with eggs.

i did not know then
what has come to me since—
that there is a signature
to all things
that which comes
without asking,
the thing given
and still un-named
like a secret
buried in complicity,
moments when we
first give fire to another
when we learn to touch,
our bodies
wrapped in a web
spun from our impermanence
our celebration.

Photo by Chris Huie

Yuri Kageyama

Yuri Kageyama was born in Aichi-ken Japan in 1953, and grew up in Tokyo, Maryland and Alabama. She is a magna cum laude graduate of Cornell University and holds a Master's degree in Sociology from the University of California, Berkeley. A performer as well, she has worked with musicians, actors and a dancer in presentations of her original works at museums, schools, cultural centers, community events and her own productions. Currently, she resides in San Francisco with her Sansei carpenter/musician husband and their one year old son Isaku.

95

Love Poem

I like
the feel of your pulsating fibers
beneath the golden muscles beneath my fingertips baby
      clams stuck against the window pane goldfish bowl
      that run soft throbs along your veins blue-pink
      rivers jutting gently against your skin against my
      skin
while I rub rub rub
your naked chest
in time and at times beats slower to our rhythm tingling
      so good
so good feelings send me out to the ozone
your hair
black black
thick, straight, glistening in the light
dark threads of seaweed bending
Asian hair
hard stubbles lining your chin
tickling
playful pine needles matsu on my lips
bounce on the roundness of my belly
curved niches between the hip bones
your eyes
are my eyes
that see and see what I have seen;
they can't ever understand
the love of a Japanese woman
who waits
pale powdered hands
eyes downcast night pools of wetness
fifteen years for her samurai lover
and when he comes back

nothing's changed
nothing's changed

A Day in a Long Hot Summer

summer of sixty-eight
hair
long red and long black
blowing in the breeze
we lie
naked
among dandelions
popping sweet and golden
shooting roots
into
blood-red
Alabamian soil;
we chew on
hot fried okra
and
smile
and smile
and
smile

last night
a VISTA worker
was beaten up bloody
for
helping fix a roof
on the wrong side of town

you wanted to
march in
Tennessee for
Doctor Martin Luther King
and
people laughed

Terry and Jim
stopping for gas
were welcomed by a
man with a shotgun,
"nigger lover!"
an Easy Rider nightmare

you whisper:
a man
bleeding by the road
sore-covered body
no arms
no legs
yet
in a glimpse
he turned
a silver kite
soaring
upwards
into the sky

Disco Chinatown

street blood throbbing
punk maggots of the slums with fake ID's
smelling British sterling
cover the stink of sweat, car grease and dirt
and the blood from being cut up by a Jo
or is it W.C.?
slant eye to slant eye talking
smooth talking or trying,
"hey, baby—
looking nice tonight"
spilling sunrises
      margaritas
      bourbons with cherries
giddy easy striding to make it to my table
in your own eyes, a ghetto knight,
"wanna drink?"
in a flash and a flick, light my cigarette,
the dance floor is dead tonight
linoleum cracked
the Filipino D.J. Berkeley Asian American Studies drop out is stoned
and even the lights look neon sleazy
you want me to move, a wax museum dancing doll, under your macho
    gaze,
or in your arms, rocking following your rocks,
layered black hair,
moustache, always, to tickle the quick kisses,
cheap shiny shirt, four buttons open,
a jade pendant swaying against yellow brown flesh,
darker brown leather and long long legs,
you want to take me home
and the grip on my shoulder tightens,
you driving a Camaro Z28?
an Olds 442?
a broken down Malibu?
a Caddy Eldorado?
you want to be rich someday
you want to enjoy life, you say,
'cuz it's so so short,
ALL girls want you for their old man,
"in bed, I have a good body,
opium makes me last

and last
I'm ten inches
and," a smile,
"this thick"
you play the mind games with a too ridiculous seriousness
not another escape out just for kicks
your street male pride can't take no scratches
you'll kick my ass when the number I give you isn't mine
you tell me not to dance with anyone else
when I just met you tonight
and isn't your old lady waiting at your apartment?
hardened hard up
Ricksha stray tiger cat
your life view quite
doesn't
touch mine
and being gang banged isn't my type of thrill
disco steps don't silence sirens
and the skyscraper lights don't touch Grant Avenue on a Friday night
Golden Dragon massacred meat can't ever be pieced back together
          again
black lights and hanging ferns or Remy sweetness can't hide
          spilled out alley fish guts
that tell you and tell you
there just ain't no future
your hands grope
your eyes closed
your tongue dry
your penis limp
poor ChinaMAN-child

Strings/Himo

orphaned
i am your child
hunger of desperation
gnawing
my brain shrinks timidly
as i sit
a Japanese ghost at the bottom of a well
trapped in the dark
waiting
waiting
waiting
for you

only
once upon a time
time was endless

i dread your touch
when you return
that melts the hurt and vengeance
of wishing
to strangle you
with your umbilical cord that
still remains
dangling
rotten smelling
a lengthy piece of dried out squid

the nymph goddess beckons from a
sung dynasty painting
plump white cheeks
porcelain fingers
streaming black hair

My Mother Takes a Bath

My mother
Sits
In the round uterine
    rippling green water
    hazy vapor-gray dampness
    soapy smelling
    in the air—a circle cloud—above
    the tub of a bath
    the wet old wood
    sending sweet stenches
    sometimes piercing to her nose and sometimes
    swimming in the hot, hot water
    tingling numb at the toes and fingertips
    when she moves too quickly but
    lukewarm caught in the folds of her white white belly
Her face is brown-spottled
    beautiful with dewdrop beads of sweat lined neatly where
        her forehead joins her black wavy tired hair
    and above her brown-pink lips
    one drop lazily hangs, droops over,
    sticking teasingly to her wrinkle
    then pling! falls gently
    playfully disappears into the water
She sighs
And touches her temple
    high and naked
    runs her fingers over the lines deep
Her hand
    has stiff knuckles
    enlarged joints crinkled and hardened
    but her thick nails thaw in the water and
    her hand is
    light
    against her face
    and gentle and knowing
    and the palm
    next to her bony thumb
    is soft
Her breasts are blue-white clear
    with soft brown nipples that dance
    floating with the movements of the .
    waves of the little ocean tub
    slowly, a step behind time, slowly
She sighs again
    thinking of her life,
    was it wasted?
    living for her husband and children?
    no, it wasn't wasted, she thinks,
    I have had a good life

to have a good husband
          such good children
This warm spot she has to herself
This warm time she has to think
She cuddles her shoulders like a fetus
          still blind, unborn
Her haunches sway
          rubbing the tub's skin
          soft brown peeling furs of wood
          little jazzed feelers in the water
Her feet are like minimized french rolls a pair
          coarse and brown on the outside
          warm, good, sweet within
She moves ever so slightly
          to go deeper into the heat
          till her neck is covered
          so
          her chin, an oversized umeboshi, barely shows
Her head sticks out
          noble
Her hands neatly
          politely
          clasped over her knees
          jutting awkward from her legs the way her elbows
                    do from her arms
Her face from the side
          the cheekbones distinct
          is an Egyptian sculpture profile
          an erotic Utamaro ukiyo-e
She sighs
Deeply
And
My Mother forgets the passing of time and ages
As she sits alone
With the water singing koto strings in her ears.

Lonny Kaneko

Lonny Kaneko is a sansei who spent his early years in Minidoka, grew up in Seattle and started writing poetry at the urging of his friend Amy Sanbo. Since then, Amy and Lonny have written a three act play, LADY IS DYING, and are currently at work on a second full length play, BENNY HANA.

Lonny's poems have been published in a variety of magazines and LADY was performed in both San Francisco and Seattle.

His latest poems were written while on a grant from the National Endowment for the Arts, 1982.

Coming Home from Camp

HER WORDS TO NO ONE   1946

It seems like the same thing all over again.
But worse. One room. Three of us in one bed,
a hot plate, sink, no refrigerator. The milk
spoils on the window sill. The bathroom's public.
I scour the tub twice. And no job.
Daddy can't find a job. He's tried.
The twenty-five they gave us as we left
the gate's not enough for rent, food, and tools.
I've tried the P.T.A. The teachers try
to be conversational. The other parents smile
and look away.
                          The farmers in Idaho
were shocked that we spoke English just like them.
They thought we'd be killers, spies who spoke
strange words and bowed a lot. We fixed
our smiles at them when they asked,
"Why have they sent you here?"
Heck, we had just as much right to be happy.
I tried to make the barrack a home and ignore
the racket the coyotes made at night.
You should have heard them. And the thunder.
In this hotel, I look out the window and see
only a brick wall four feet away.
No sky. I guess Camp wasn't so bad. At least
we had a yard, even if the fence was there
to keep us in. The menfolk learned to make
tables and chairs, and toys like Mickey Mouse
and Pluto. I learned to embroider flowers and birds
on a branch.
                          Here there's the whine of cars and howls
from trains grinding into the station night
after night.   There's no reason to say,
"Things will get better." Daddy's got to try harder.
But he won't. Or can't. I never knew
this side of him. After a while you realize
that nothing changes. You don't say, "Keep trying."
You know that nothing changes. It just repeats.
And then you stop. You don't know when it happens.
But it does.

Goddamit, she doesn't want to do anything.
She's locked herself in the house and won't go out.
I tell her, "Let's go visit," but she won't.
"Don't have a thing to wear," she insists. "Buy
a dress," I say. "It's a waste," she says, "to cut
twelve inches off a dress to make it fit.
And children's clothes—never."
                              After twelve hours
of work, I feel like company when I get home.
Some nights I walk to the drugstore to chew the fat.
I know, I promised to fix the house. It's better
than the old hotel, but needs cupboards and a furnace.
The oil heater's okay. I cut a hole
in the ceiling to heat upstairs, but it's not enough
when it snows. The kid's had mumps, tonsilitis
and measles for two months straight. We cross our fingers
and hope.
                    She keeps ten years of *Life* in piles,
ten years of *Look, Better Homes and Gardens,*
Good Housekeeping, and now a stack of *Family Circle.*
All we do is eat and read the paper.

Before the war she'd shake the doors with me
in Chinatown. You call it Security:
when the shops were closed, we'd go down and make sure.
Got shot once in the leg while eating *udon.*
Saw a Chinaman wave a gun. We slid
behind a table, and I drew mine, but he shot
and ran. Think that's why they gave me a badge
at Camp. Made me captain, because I carried
a gun and kept my peace.
                              Now I hope there's work
to get us through the week. I hope for something
steadier than cutting grass in summer rain
and bleeding chicken in the snow. Then I think,
it's just as well. I'd hate to lose it all
again. There's less to lose like this. No choice
in those days. Everywhere I looked they said,
"Sorry, you're too old." I was forty-two
and strong enough to last another twenty.
Hell, the truth is they wouldn't trust this Jap
to keep a parking lot full of cars. It's enough
to keep this house. What can you do but hope
you'll change so they won't say *no.* That's the magic
word, *Change.* You hope it's better for you. You hope
it's better for your son. That's why you work.
You hope or die.

SON'S WORDS TO HIS TEENAGE CHILDREN   1982

I go alone into the rain, as you must,
a thousand miles from me, past the sagging buildings
where Ba-chan still insists is home, trying to keep
her dying house alive, now Ji-chan's dead.
When I was young, their voices, incessant and empty,
collapsed across the dinner table.
Fear like a .38 followed us from Minidoka.
Worn out and rusty, they sat there cornered
by their own silence. It's as easy to close out
the world as it is to latch a door. The mind dies
in a silence of its own making, and action is chained
by a lock of fear which strangles like a braid
of one's own waistlength hair. Every decision
becomes an unanswerable stutter.

As a child I dozed among the canteloupes unaware
of barbed wire and guns. Today the Minidoka-response lives
in me, passed from mother and father on to son.
There's an animal chained inside, wordless as a bird.

I want you unchained and memorable.
The best gift is freedom. My eyes measure
the chains of this world. The electric fence contains
the fearful; but the mind outleaps loneliness and despair.
I cannot do more than I believe I can.
Like a lake, my own shore despairs the air's freedom,
but the ocean breaks and recedes, its face
an unalterable tide.

I've quit breathing life into lifeless words
that won't stand up and walk. I throw myself
into stoneware, shape and reshape the mindless goo,
trying to find something familiar there.
I'm worn out, rusty from the uncomfortable rain.
This is my gift: we've come a long way from camp;
sometimes like the broken pieces of a stoneware jar,
we're scattered across the floor and forced to make
ourselves at home, wherever we happen to be.

The Secret

In memory of Sanny Kaneko 1905–1980

"I heard him fall. He's lying
on the floor," my mother's voice
repeats the words
that carried across the continent.
"Cold when I touched him."
He's gone.
"The ambulance . . ."
My father's dead.
It's been a year.
I spit the words
and the secret's out.
The garden's gone seedy.
Even the compost knows.
The star magnolia and wisteria, too.
They miss him like a sharp wind
or a thunder shower.

The secret's out.
I wanted him to die
when he was ready,
so I could take his place.
But it's too late,
the spider webs the corners
of his room. My mother lives
with my father's death. He's still
preserved in his wedding solemnity
on her buffet, or laughing
after forty years, about to catch
the ball my mother's tossed. Every night
she feeds his photograph, too busy
with habit to understand
that feeding a man is not
her only freedom.

The truth is, she won't let him die.
She stuffed him into a cardboard box
and trapped him there.
My heart staggers as his did,
like a drunk spider on a loose thread
against my ribs.
I ignore it until she decides
I should fill his place
behind the wheel of his car
or at the table behind the
Sunday sports page,
my elbows propped like his.

I feel my heart wheeze,
know that I am dying inside,
but I can't let him die either.
I hold him here in my hands—
this skin, nails, no eyes to cry,
muscles that work these words.
"If the ambulance was there on time ..."
my mother remembers.
Our words work a web around us.
They house our grief.

Father, this is no good night.
Good bye.   Good bye.

Violets for Mother

I hear my mother whose hips have
broadened sadly rocking in the chair
that she has reglued and tied together
twice these past five years.
She is staring through the living room,
older than her mother, her eyes fixed
on the glass that conveys the light and shade
of days.   They are quiet now, straight lines
of sunlight that arrow to certainty and fear
enough to strap one to a rocking chair
for days on end as when she rocked me for ten
and my sister for some twenty years.
Now she rocks all my brothers, unborn
either through abstinence or luck.
Oh, that we could walk to her side or look into her face
and say that we love her
a chorus of our voices from Minidoka to Seattle
without unsettling the jungle
of African violets steaming quietly around her,
and in whose presence love
whispers its pink flowers.

Family Album

for Charlotte Davis

1939

Picture my grandmother at sixty the year
I was born standing in an old wooden tub
amazed by the shrunken fruit of her breasts,
the dry blossom ends of her nipples
soaking in steamy water.
A slender thread slips through the dark
of her skull like a snake and the room spins
and water rises past her arm pits, sweeping
over her like a wave of sunlight.

1940

My grandfather stands in half-drained peat
puzzling over the jigsaw of her face
that lies like firewood behind the house.
When three inch corn and beans wilt from a late frost
he sails back to Japan where earth, he says,
is civilized.   He dies ten years later
50 miles northeast of Hiroshima.

1942

The locomotive steams over names like Puyallup,
Boise, Twin Falls, and Burley; it heads
where men throw nails and two-by-fours
into desert air.   They fall into long lines.
Soldiers empty the cars of names
like Naganawa, Namba, Hiroshige
and prod faces named George, Linc, or Naomi
into rooms furnished with sawdust and sage.

The sign says MINIDOKA.
Nobody knows what it means.

1943

My mother waits in line for the laundry tub
she will wash me in; I wait in line naked
while lightning worms through July.
I wait in the midst of our people who say,
"You'll lose your thumbs if you don't eat your crusts."
and show me hands without thumbs.

A snake winds its way under the sun,
unconcerned, eternal.   And the sun drinks us up,
like the earth across the yard, never quenched.

1945

Past the gates on our way out,
I see where the water waits.
It is *Minidoka* dam,
a place for holding the snake
before it falls
into another country.

1965

A king apple's limbs scratch the sky.
The barn sits like a beached whale;
it will survive the next flood and winter
because it is already dead.
Grandfather's house sags with wrinkles,
is tattered with weather.

My father in this country
wears rubber boots
to keep out the blood and water.
But he has grown old, too.
The chickens he bleeds
string across the Pacific.
They scrape down stainless steel belts
to be feathered and return nude,
bottoms up, their bellies empty.

1973

Yesterday Charlotte asked, "Is there still
a bitterness? Something wormed its way through my blood.
Snake. Water. Earth. "It is a thirst," I say.

Today, in the library a reference book
says that *Minidoka* means water.
Water. Something we choke on.

Joy Kogawa

Joy Kogawa born Joy Nozomi Nakayama in Vancouver, B.C., Canada on June 6, 1935. 2 children, Gordon and Deidre. Written 3 volumes of poetry—all out of print. The Splintered Moon, *U. of New Brunswick, 1967,* A Choice of Dreams, *1974 McClelland & Stewart,* Jericho Road, *McClelland & Stewart, 1977. Writer-in-residence at University of Ottawa 1978. First novel* Obasan, *1981, Lester & Orpen Dennys, Canada; 1982 David Godine U.S.; Futami Shoho 1983 Japan; Penguin Canada 1983. Obasan won Books in Canada first novel award; Canadian Authors Association Book of the Year award; Before Columbus Foundation American Book Award; Chosen as a notable book by American Library Association, selected by Book of the Month Club and Literary Guild.*

Book of poems Woman in the Woods *forthcoming.*

Ancestors' Graves in Kurakawa

Down down across the open sea to Shikoku
To story book island of mist and mystery
By train and bus through remote mountain villages
Following my father's boyhood backwards
Retracing the mountain path he crossed on rice husk slippers
With his dreams of countries beyond seas beyond seas
His dreams still intact, his flight perpetual
Back down the steep red mountain path
To the high hillside grave of my ancestors
Grey and green ferns hang down
Edging my faint beginnings with shades
Maintaining muteness in a wordless flickering
The hiddenness stretches beyond my reach
Strange dew drops through cedar incense
And I greet the dead who smile through trees
Accepting the pebbles that melt through my eyes.

On Meeting the Clergy
of the Holy Catholic Church in Osaka

Heralded into a belly swelling bladder bloating banquet
Where the excessive propriety is hard on the digestion
Elegant ladies in kimonos and holy men with holier manners
Bow and re-bow in strict pecking order
Munch the meal and mouth polite belching and
Rush at flood tide to the integrated toilet
Where men still proper and black suited in a row
Stand toes out and eyes down in syncopated gush
While ladies in kimonos mince by without blush or bellow
And I follow snuffling to hide a guffaw though
Why should I laugh—which reminds me
At the Osaka zoo my friend kept pointing out
The peeing fox and the baboon's purple bum and such
Asking how to say these things in English
And I tried to explain about the odd Canadians
Who have no bread and butter words
To describe these ordinary things.

Hiroshima Exit

In round round rooms of our wanderings
Victims and victimizers in circular flight
Fact pursuing fact
Warning leaflets still drip down
On soil heavy with flames,
Black rain, footsteps, witnessings—

The Atomic Bomb Memorial Building:
A curiosity shop filled with
Remnants of clothing, radiation sickness,
Fleshless faces, tourists muttering
"Well, they started it."
Words jingle down
"They didn't think about us in Pearl Harbor"
They? Us?
I tiptoe around the curiosity shop
Seeking my target
Precision becomes essential
Quick. Quick. Before he's out of range
Spell the name
America?
Hiroshima?
Air raid warnings wail bleakly
Hiroshima
Morning.
I step outside
And close softly the door
Believing, believing
That outside this store
Is another door

Dream after Touring the Tokyo Tokei

Electronic baby born to be
Guide in clock manufacturing hospital
Son of General Secretary of Resurrection
With a white bib on cold steel chest
Comes sliding squealing into this world
Ready to perform his single task
And guides me, ancient earthling
Through metal spot after metal spot
Where oil, like blood, alive, is flowing and
Small steel birds beep through the air
Carrying messages of cheer to the ill—
"Behold, before you were born I was here."
I reach out and am electrocuted
And the steel baby within me leaps—
Oh be born quickly before my flesh is Sarah grey
That I might see the shape of ancient promise

We step outside to Tokyo twentieth century
Seeds of slaves drift down from factory windows
And settle in the branches of dwarf trees
Settle on metal ledges and in the streets
Drop like confetti over the rose garden
And inside the bonnet of an opening rose
On the wrinkled old woman face of the bud
Stands a stiff black beetle on steely legs
An ancient wedding procession begins
In the dusty rose garden by the Tokyo Tokei.

Every spot is a sliding oil spot
And though I might seek to stay in this dream forever
I am sliding constantly in a procession.
Even at the moment of forgetting
An undercurrent has slid me further along.
Clandestine flesh and steel meetings
Move towards unions
And beyond this another resurrection.

Woodtick

The spring day the teen on his bike slanted his caucasian eyes
At my eight year old beautiful daughter
And taunted gibberish
I was eight years old and the Japs were
Enemies of Canada and the big white boys
And their golden haired sisters who
Lived in the ghost town of Slocan
Were walking together, crowding me
Off the path of the mountain, me running
Into the forest to escape
Into the pine brown and green lush dark
And getting lost and fearing woodticks
Which burrowed into your scalp beneath
Thick black hair follicles and could only be
Dug out by a doctor with hot needles—
Fearing sudden slips caused by melting snow
And steep ravines and the thick silence of
Steaming woods and cobwebs, so listening
For the guiding sound of their laughter
To lead me back to the path and
Following from a safe distance unseen
Till near the foot of the mountain
Then running past faster than their laughter
Home, vowing never to go again to the mountain
Alone—and Deidre whispers to walk faster
Though I tell her there are no
Woodticks in Saskatoon.

Tina Koyama

Recipe for Bread

(for G.C.)

When I was taking a breadbaking class, I learned two important things. The first is how *not* to follow recipes. I began the class taking careful notes, asking my teacher questions like, "How much honey did you just add?" and always getting answers like, "A glob or so," and feeling silly writing that down. I soon gave up the notebook, and with each loaf I baked, I learned to trust the feel of the dough that told me to add more flour or water or to knead it a little longer. I grew adventurous, throwing in a banana here or maybe more buttermilk there. Some loaves turn out better than others, I admit, but each is different and a chance to try something new. For the best bread comes not from precisely measuring 6¾ cups of flour according to a cookbook but comes instead from following a recipe that's always changing, the one in my hands and heart.

The second thing I learned is about myself. I like fresh bread for dinner, with lots of butter and jam. I like wrapping a warm loaf in my mother's cotton fukin and bringing it to a friend or neighbor. What I love most, though, is not the bread but the making—the sharp smell of yeast filling the kitchen as I knead; being wrist-deep in sticky dough when the phone rings and letting it ring; watching the dough rise and wanting to hurry it along but just the same leaving it alone. The making is what keeps me attentive, always adding to the dough or getting my hands in it or simply waiting for it. The first slice is barely cut and tasted and already I'm thinking of what I'll do different, and better, with the next loaf.

Writing poems is just like this.

Grape Daiquiri

*"You were forty years too late
to be having your first drink."*

—*Richard Koyama*

Your cousin tells you it's like fruit juice,
what she always orders, and you let
the cool sweetness deceive your thirst,
placate your grumbling stomach.

At first you hardly notice the faces
moving in and out of focus,
the room lights dimming. Three sips more
and a waiter's white sleeve dissolves like sugar.
Beside you, your husband speaks from the far end
of a tunnel, repeating another fish-story
between gulps of his third V.O.-and-water.

You want to warn them—these smiling,
bobbing heads around the table—
warn them of the dangers, that the walls
melt and fall like icing on a cake,
but you know they won't hear you
for the droning of bees between your ears.
You try to shake them free, but the floor
sifts like flour beneath your feet.
A chair fools you into thinking it's steady.
Bees pour honey down your eyes,
pull the color from your cheeks
and let it pool in the pockets of your knees.

Trying to remember when you've felt this way
before, you recall the thick sweetness of ether
smelled once for each daughter and son.
Curious, the things you think of last:
your children in another city, eating
ice cream or reading novels; a photo
of your mother framed above your desk;
the purple of the carpet as it rises
to soften your fall.

Definitions of the Word *Gout*

In Japanese,
two characters combine:
Wind.
Pain.

A man sits in his easy chair,
stares at his big toe, watches it swell
to the size of a lemon,
glow red as tuna sashimi.
At each meal, his wife
reminds him what he can't have:
acids, maguro, tea spiked with V.O.
Increase alkalinity, says his friend
at Lloyd's Boathouse.
Avoid beans.

From the patio door, a Rainier wind
whitens lake water on the other side
of the bridge, pulls my mother's
haiku calendar from the wall.
She comes in to close the door,
replace the calendar,
reach a corncob pipe for my father.
Shifting his weight to light
the pipe, he is careful not to jar
the big toe. Through his pipe,
he breathes out the last of the wind
as if it were a word.

Ojisan After the Stroke: Three Notes to Himself

(for my uncle)

Early morning.
Small birds drop from the plum tree
to the yard. Every day, their patterns
in my window the same: my window
always the same.

Afternoon.
Voices from the kitchen buzz in
and out of the room. I catch my name
in the corners like too much light.
Wasted as my left side.

Night.
The moon is half empty,
but I can't remember
if it's growing or shrinking. It creeps out
of my window
and into the rest of darkness.

Next

Probing my mouth as if searching for gold,
eyeing the lower left molar, his raw, unpolished jewel,
the man with snaps on his shoulder leans into me, so
eager I'm surprised he doesn't jump
right in, take a dip in cool pools of saliva.

"Keep it open, please," he smiles, then asks about my dog,
undergraduate education, the muffler on my car,
smiling, always smiling, his kind moon eyes expecting
answers. He knows my life can be answered with a nod,
knows the stoney surface of my tooth
and the narrow parabola of my jaw
better than his own hand. He fears
extraction will be necessary, taps with his mirror

deep cracks that even promises won't fill. Here,
decisions come in the shape of pliers. I nod,
swallowing old questions with a numbing tongue.

Photo by Ken Pate

Geraldine Kudaka

Born in Hawaii, 1951, the daughter of Ronald Shojin Kudaka and Sadako Awakuni Kudaka. Received a short formal education at SJSU and UCLA. Considers herself molten of self-cast metal. Of the independent new breed. Since 1969 has worked freelance as a camerawoman/filmaker. Travelled to Cuba, Mexico, Japan, Hong Kong, and both East and West Coast of the United States.

In between, she was one of the founders of Third World Communications, an editor of Third World Women's Book, a poet-teacher for Poetry In The Schools, and poet on the CETA Program. She has been published in numerous magazines and anthologies.

Okinawa Kanashii Monogatari

okinawa kanashii monogatari
the bird has been chained
to the sky
its tether stretching the pacific
crucified between the u.s. and jieitai
okinawa, okinawa
i who have loved you for so long
i weep for you
            for you were the laughter
of my land
the island of smiles/ valleys of tears
okinawa
okinawa kanashii monogatari
until the rain sweeps away the tears
i am blind
until the voices of the dead
burn the asphalt jungles
            okinawa kaiyo
until the rain sweeps away the tears
i am blind
until the voices of the dead
burn the asphalt jungles
            okinawa kaiyo
until a hundred men become a thousand
            ampo funsai/ ampo funsai
until the machines which convert
time into pain/ fields into graves
creak and rust into the past
            there will be no songs
bird wings clipped, birds feet chained

On Writing Asian-American Poety

Takamura Kotaro
speaks
of fireplaces
ancient magpie homes
where
Chieko lived

> my mixed up
> poems
> are hybrid races:
> an american birth

Takahashi Mutsuo
knows
of minos, pungent sex,
male tongues,
and sturdy legs

> under a terrible
> sunrise
> my grandparents
> came to america

Shiraishi Kazuko
swirls cocks
and shadows
into statuesque carvings

> we ate rice
> and langendorf bread
> plates of
> *padded bras, blondes,*
> *John Wayne, pigs n tofu*

shinkansen trains rush by
transporting kimono bodies
in suits and ties

> we said the pledge
> of allegiance
> and learned english
> as a 2nd language

outside new york
there is a
blizzard blazing

i invited you over
& fed you tea
behind coy hands you
snickered

Ne chotto suifu-san
Umi kara agatta bakari no

you took my poems
you took my soul
your hands rusty hangers
aborting my child

we learned racism
& believed
blondes had more fun

you became the judge
and i condemned
your lily white suburbs
and i ghetto splattered

my tempura-kim chi menu
spilled on tatami mat
my black hair black eyes
scan your proper stance

Asakawa Maki
jazz priestess of
japaaan
wails Langston Hughes

Ne chotto suifu-san
Umi kara agatta bakari no

in america
did the vastness
of camps
feed
myopic vision?

Birthright

i am the crazy woman
who killed her mother
i wear nikon lenses
for eyes
and lie thru the skin
of my teeth
nicotineo rows alined by
braces
locks, and window fixtures
i go crazy stripping
off wallpaper
i paint my nails red
i leave the lover
i loved most,
send postcards
from the coast, little
notes saying
"on the way to the embassy
i lost my smile ..."
i like strange men
whose intimacy
gives them power
i write without alliance
i take on improbability
with the fury
of a hellcat and rub
my silk collar
against my nose
i am the crazy woman
who is not
so crazy after all
i lied when i said
i killed my mother
in my womb, i am carrying her
our birthright fur
blood & spit ...

Death is a Second Cousin Dining with Us Tonight

The night is warm and hot, my arms
are sticky. I call you in.
On an old formica table, dinner
is a half cooked slab of meat.
We sit and chew silently.
Your hair is dirty. Three years ago,
it was pitch black night
an unending line that flew in the wind.

My eye twitches mercilessly.
I won't look up.
The walls are closing in. One of us
will have to break the silence.
A pale moth beats the table lamp.
It's wings are burned.
It won't go anywhere. In my hand, the bent fork
grinds the potatoes
into kingdoms rising, falling. . .

The year was 1976. Our only son
played near the drain.
When he would do those things, afterwards,
I'd hold him tight to my breast.
That time he climbed onto the roof
of a deserted barn, I cried and cried.
When you got home, the smell of rubble hung
off your carefully patched hands.

Lifting up my head, I meet your eyes.
Your thick, fat fingers dig into the tabletop.
Knocking the empty chair aside, you swear
"God DAMN IT!! Stop playing with your food!"
You won't say it, but your hands
are ready to choke the words out of me.

The dull thud in my ears is a pale body
beating the bulb. I reached over.
My dried finger knocks the moth aside.
The powdery wings flutter. On the yellow speckled
formica, the wings frantically beat.
I can't help myself, the silence of the air
is pregnant with company.

I lift a forkful of boiled potatoes to my mouth.
In a calm voice, I ask you if you want some bread.

Giving Up Butterflies

Fresno, 1948

The others stand in their imported
ready-made wear.
I stand apart, my carefully dressed hair
coiffed above a starched, white dress.

I suck in my stomach,
pulling flat the tell-tale months,
that single moment
when mattress springs dug into my back.

i.

The placenta came out intact.
I had bruises for months afterwards.
The necklace you gave me hung off my door,
the shimmering light that danced off
was all that you left.

ii.

Under a barren walnut tree,
my shovel propped up the newborn bark.
I sat staring at the empty hole, the corn
flour sack, and that morning's paper.

For months on end, I sat rocking time
back and forth.
The shell of my life cracked into two distinct
moments, back and forth.
Back and forth.

My bare soles rubbed one spot
on the rickety floor. My arms were
hard and stiff, my legs bare and hollow.
I rocked,
waiting for god knows what,
back and forth.

iii.

My mother screamed, "Turn off the water!
What do you think we are? Rich?"
Clicking the lock in place, I paid her no
attention.

I waited until she left, then dressed
in my Sunday best.
Standing on the porch, I caught a butterfly
and tore off its wings.
I buried its wings under the maple tree.
The dull sparkles in the cold, brown soil
forgot to shine.

iv.

Inside my body, an unknown surgeon
has cauterized my pride.
My hurt betrays me. I can't look
up, my eyes are glued to the polished
oak, the leather shoes.

The smoking laughter of the crowd fills
the air with an unpleasant
smell, You glide by, your feet so
swift, so sure,
packs my heart into a tiny earthen knot.

With one hand covering my eyes, the other
carrying my pride, I walk out.
In the autumn night, I feel the frost
of winter.
Soon it will be spring.

Photo by Zoe Filipkowski

Alex Kuo

Always hesitant to say much here. Except, living in Moscow, Idaho, and writes and hunts a lot. The Window Tree *(1971), and* New Letters from Hiroshima and Other Poems *(1974). Have four books looking for publisher/s, including a children's book and a collection of short fiction. That is my statement.*

Did You Not See

the aspens yesterday
intolerant and drawn
together high up on the Divide?

Perhaps you gave them a glance
gazing out the high window
in the back of your house
saw nothing and now
remember nothing more?

What did the second settlers
see when they first stumbled
up these yellowed tiers
trying to find their way to
the Pacific, their senses drying
in that October trying
to change their significance?

Perhaps now you can remember
their prints in that early ice
how they packed along their dead
until the ground was soft
enough for late burial
step after step
disappearing high into
this incomprehensible blue.

Loss

It all began
with my fingers pressing
into the small
of your naked

back, or with yours
into mine when
(then) we both
moved moving against

each other's flesh
against the snow
under us, under
the snow melting

into the shape
of our bodies, as
did our hands
into, too

the shape of each
other's back. Or
was it the other
way around, with

the eccentric sense
of time
and place receding
beyond their abstract

in my present
knowing. I don't know
which for sure
now, or whether it

even ever
happened at all
then. Experience is
the hard loss

of language
and place beyond
time
(now) the impossible

location of a past
I can claim
no understanding
of, no, not

now, or then
of then returning
there, dying
there in the beginning.

An Early Illinois Winter

What is left in field
after field after fall's reaping

will be collected in some neurotic
scrapbook: bits of broken

wings, clumps of black
dirt gutted with roots

the machines could not take
a squashed *Schlitz* can thrown

out by some passing motorist.
My boots knock down

last night's first
frost and crush it under

my steps. What is it that stirs
this air and pushes it to sheer

exhaustion so late in coming?
Nobody's around anywhere.

I repeat asking to myself
the question whose answer I know.

On A Clear Day I Can See Forever

once there was an old lady who sat in her
window i saw her there for three days in
the same chair with the same smile i went
in the next day and she was dead

i am not surprised

i will poison the photographers
with my hereditary claim

i will leave statements
on her unmarked grave

i will swing from trees
and keep away the pilgrims

i will sit in her window
and watch the day go down

i will gather all her things
and burn them in the night

then i will sit in the dark
and wait there forever

i will say nothing

There is Something I Want to Say

Not a sound to pull
the world into new shapes:

silence waits
on puddles and puddles.

The lake lies languid
through the rectangular window

and the festering sunlight
becomes paralytic.

And the butchers
have wiped their dead furniture

clean and christmas
with us:

starry meals:
tables balloon with meat

and sugar
(mine squeaks like a funny

pink cat.)
But my mother

did you hear her
heart beating in

the ocean
with fierce courage?

Potato block print by Alan Chong Lau

Alan Chong Lau

Alan Chong Lau was born in Oroville, California and grew up in Paradise, a small town in the upper Sacramento valley. He received his B.A. in Art from the University of California at Santa Cruz in 1976. His work has appeared in many literary magazines and anthologies including Yardbird Reader III, Califia *edited by Ishmael Reed (I. Reed Press),* The Next World *edited by Joseph Bruchac (Crossing Press),* Heartland *edited by Gerald Haslam and James Houston (Capra Press),* Amerasia Journal *and the forthcoming,* The Big Aiiieeeee: Asian American History in Literature *edited by Jeffrey Paul Chan, Frank Chin, Lawson Inada and Shawn Wong (Howard University Press). In 1976 he was recipient of a special projects grant from the California Arts Council and in 1979 the King County Arts Commission Publication Grant in Poetry as judged by Ishmael Reed and Kay Boyle. Along with poets Lawson Inada and Garrett Hongo and by himself, he has toured the West Coast doing poetry readings with music in Canada, Washington and California. Lau is also a visual artist presently showing at the Francine Seders Gallery in Seattle. His publications include* Buddha Bandits Down Highway 99 *with Lawson Inada and Garrett Hongo (Buddha-head Press) and* Songs For Jadina *(Greenfield Review Press).* Songs From Jadina *received the American Book Award from the Before Columbus Foundation in 1981. In 1982 he served as co-editor with Mayumi Tsutakawa for an anthology entitled* Turning Shadows Into Light: Art and Culture of the Northwests Early Asian/Pacific Community *(Young Pine Press). Most recently he is co-editing a special Asian American poetry issue of Contract II magazine with Laureen Mar which will feature poetry and reviews by Asian American poets of North and South America. He is a recipient of a Creative Artist Fellowship for Japan for 1982-83.*

crossing portsmouth bridge

for grandmother and teru

"the portsmouth bridge is a cement overpass erected by the
holiday inn and goes into portsmouth square, a park in the
heart of san francisco's chinatown"

over the bridge
your ghost
dries chicken wings
stretched across
a newspaper in october

so hot
the characters
dance
like a shimmer
of black ants
around food

each wing
well preserved
fingers of some child
embalmed
from a dynasty we never knew
or a boy shot dead in the street

with red twine
from bakery boxes
you fashion a necklace
for me to wear

i try to tell you
though a chicken
has wings
it cannot fly
but only flaps dust
into the eyes of ants

nothing i say
convinces

each wing
becomes a finger
attached to a hand

the twine
a line of blood
a circle
to connect memory to bone

we give
each of our lives
a name
and wear it

crossing this bridge
of cement
we enter a foreign land

these necklaces
our only proof
that we were never
here

father takes to the road and lets his hair down

my father
lets his hair down now
days when he called me "yeepie"
all but forgotten

it peeps over
the collar
shyly asks permission
to grow

while the center
of his head shines
as each year
more is revealed

now when he drives
signs no longer deserve attention
no right/left or railroad crossing

stranded on a fork
between roads
he'd rather talk to mother
in chinese
forget about time
and the lantern of a patrol car
at our back

pick his teeth
with a toothpick
nudge out slivers of fish
and sing this song
he once heard in another village

*(sunday february 27, 1983 — a few days after
the death of 13 people in seattle's chinatown)*

day of the parade

1
the first truckload
jars sleep loose
nappa from california
insists its importance
with this crate flecked with mud
and stamped with a single bootprint

the light in the fields
forces worms to hide
in this boxed shade
overgrown
stalks come out of hearts
layers of leafy veins
converge into a mush of pus
that smears my apron

today's shoppers lack excitement
circle past oranges
at six pounds for a dollar
ignore the presence
of a tangled chorus of beansprouts
that sing water
resist the temptation to stroke
long white legs of daikon
instead repeat a refrain
underscored by muzak
"when's the chinatown parade
do you know?"

2
an empty tour bus
runs over the offering
of vegetables arranged on a sidewalk
to appease the lion

already people
anticipating the parade
maneuver the bricks of hing hay park
strewn with tossed leftovers
for pigeons and seagulls

it doesn't matter
whether it's good cheap food
or dots of blood
that blemish a doorway
some peer down the alley
where police stumbled
"into a sea of blood"

Alan Chong Lau 137

3
the next morning
nobody i talked to
knew there was a parade
some only saw it as a dream
coming into their living rooms
on the evening news
to rob their sleep

all over this city
other people fill space
empty of curiosity
mourn a loss
that silences the ground
where no offerings can ever penetrate
no birds can ever settle

what *is* real
repeats itself 13 times
reverberates through families
an unwanted history
burning in an unlit closet
for generations to choke on

letters from kazuko (kyoto, japan — Summer 1980)

1
i see you
in the darkest recess
of this house
cupped in shadow

that room by a garden
fanning away mosquitoes

2
outside your window
a baby   a mother   a boy
breathe together pushing
the bicycle moves
by itself

"she carries her life with her"
you say

3
in the public bath
the firm breasts
of a 16 year old look mature

but when her mother scolds
she giggles
the blush of a peach

4
"the word
space
in english feels empty
but here space
is a place being filled"

5
after a storm
the mobile starts to dance

holding this pen
by a window
you bend over and write

"because of the rain
yesterday and today
the sky becomes cool
outside i feel cicadas
shaking the air around me"

living in the world

my mother thinks
it's a vietnamese family
that lives in 2 B
but the black curtains
fading to gray
haven't opened once
not even voices of ghosts
are heard

a man down the hall
employed with sorrow
scoops up empty time
and knocks on the door
once a week with *watchtower*
a magazine he says
will save the world

the manager wants
to give your twelve year old
shooting demonstrations
coos about his gun collection
like the names of women
he can fondle and touch
"i usta be a salesman
for remington rand
it's the jews and the niggers
i can't stand
but orientals are *good* people"

a week ago
you turned down his invitation
to hear george wallace records
over mogen david
sprawled on a couch

but tonight all is calm
the american has not locked
his korean wife
out of the house

the silver skeletons
of shopping carts drowned
in the swimming pool
have disappeared

in the laundramat
no circular ballet of dust
finds music
because no one feeds it coins
or crams its overfed mouth
with a week of sweat and diapers

so we talk into the night
until the star spangled banner
fades from view and
a white blip burns
the heart of the tube

undaunted
you reach for a talk show
alone in rooms
of the same city
voices come together around a radio
in a chain letter of call and response

when the signal fades
to static snow
the hum of a heater
lulls you to snoring

outside
the moon fades
into a 7/11
the only light on the block

Photo and makeup by Lynn DeBon, Hair: Shannon

Deborah Lee

In trying to describe myself and background, nothing cute or clever comes to mind to say, so I'll just give you the facts. I was born on Mother's Day, 1954, in Seattle, WA to a Chinese father and mother of undetermined white nationalities, who has always worn her hair black, could pass for Chinese, and did learn to swear in Cantonese. I grew up on Beacon Hill with 4 sisters, all younger, all of us 2 years apart in age. I overcame extreme shyness at 15 and had a baby girl at 16. At 18 I was a supporter of causes, especially concerning women's rights, and looked a bit like Buffy St. Marie. I began college that same year, the University of Washington, and I am not sure that I have stopped yet. I got a B.A. in English Literature, a B.A. in Art History, and am currently on-leave from graduate school, 3 classes short of a masters in creative writing. I lived in N.Y. and Connecticut for 1½ years with my daughter, just for a change, but the northwest is our home. Though I still find wandering enjoyable. I work full-time as the coordinator of the county Prosecutor's Victim Assistance Unit, Juvenile Division. I write when I can.

Where He Hangs His Hat

(for KB)

I.

It's a box of furniture in a right angle
with a view. No matter how
drunk, following his beer bottle,
a man behind a leash, he's pulled
home. Though he does have trouble
remembering the facts, which, like his keys,
are always under something.

This is the dream where undisguised
he tells himself:
> Leaving is as simple as clearing my throat.
> If I were happy I'd never come back.

II.

He knows who he is. The mail arrives
to remind him. All the Dear Sirs keep him
company at the table, ask Are You There?

He looks into his drink and imagines
living behind a waterfall
where the only dark spots are fish.

III.

When the dishes obscure the sink
he saves jars to drink from.
Their lids lie in clusters
on the windowledge like shells.
The garbage bags left like sagging
potatoes, grow soft and slump
against each another.
Look for no vacancies here.
The envelopes mound
like spilled flour
and cupboards open as false doors
to walls of beer bottles,
empties bricked in 6-pack cartons.
Rosetta, the living philodendron,
heads up the wall, splitting leaves
toward the door.

These are daily facts, as the black
and white of papers that pad the livingroom,
as the news that doesn't recycle
but is insulation, like forgetting.

Bare-headed, this must be home
where a man, unwatched, can swing
into his own dance, a free
step and snap in any direction.
Where the falling is soft.

You're Sorry, Your Mother is Crazy, & I'm a Chinese Shiksa

(to Sid)

I read it in the restroom, in pink nail polish:
Jews are good lays. If I continued
the graffiti, I'd diagram your slump,
a punched bag.
I'd note; this is the condition of exhaling
familiar air; just follow the curve around
half a generation. I'd add;
these arrows indicate pressure points
along the spine where the nerves, the blood lines
most feel the pinch. Circled;
guilt is the pump at the center
and the finger
points to heritage at the top,
in the brain and inevitable baldness.

Let's pause just a moment for Sundays, for the paper
passed over breakfast and the coupons
torn and compared. My savings include
your explanations on kosher meat, on being
the only son and thirty,
on why family functions are best
when avoided. And didn't you give me the memory
of your dog Schnapps, your mother's shoe
in his mouth, the screech in hers biting off
your excuses? There is the picture of your father, his smile
not pictured, and your sister with ratted hair
always ducking away. And can't I imagine you
at six, sitting alone on the front steps, waiting
and snapping at flies with cupped hands?

Goodbye in Yiddish to you and your Jewish mother,
your grandmother, translated: Spare me the Chinese!
and to your father who does not know me
but thanks you for leaving him out of it.

We leave each other
to slough off the obvious, so much
outerwear. It is a decision and here
are no pictures of me to hide.
When did you notice
that time for us skipped and stopped, a sniffing
three-legged stray?

WOMEN
OPEN CAUTIOUSLY

—from a door in Suzzallo Library,
University of Washington

Here they are. Think of it.
You are warned of women
and the term is less specific
than your fantasies. True,
they may wait beside
cushioned couches, poised with grapes
and wanting you. But what if
they're all on telephones, talking
about you, calling you clumsy
& quick, saying your hands
grip everything like the wheel
though you can't tell where
you're going? Consider the faces
of women, they're there,
theoretical as money. Yes,
it's this way to the wonderful women—
and don't forget the ruby words,
store them in your cheeks
like nuts, for when
they will say they love you
and you must say it back.

Words from a Bottle

for Gloria

I.
The refrigerator slams
and she's back in her chair;
eyes like an interrogator,
blowing smoke in my face.
I watch the ashes burn,
approaching her fingers—
think of those old fireworks
looking like licorice bits,
the grey curling ashes
like snakes sprouting.
I think we called them snakes.
I called her Medusa.

II.
Wine, she said, kept her regular
but scotch kept her happy.
Tonight she stares
through a burgundy flush.

III.
You know all you kids are pretty
damn good. I did the right thing,
having all five of you;
picked the right man
for your father.
He could never handle money
but he could handle kids.
Do you know what saves him
from being an alcoholic?
He loves to eat.
Loves all his own cooking—
all that greasy roast pork
and skillets of fried rice, chow mein—
him with that belly like a Buddha.
And do you know what saves me?
Two kids still in high school
and the back taxes he left.

IV.
She unwinds the scarf at her neck
like a bandage,
drops it across her lap—
a rayon/silk napkin
twirled around the fingers
of the non-smoking hand.
I call her mother;
she with the smile set hard
wincing, don't get old like me,
me with only one word left;
survive.

Taking Care of It

That's my house with the red door, and all those steps
lead to it. The rockery is serious grey today,
I can't see the hens and chickens or elephant ears.
My dress has two rows of ruffles down the front
and lace all around.
My shiny round-toed shoes keep tapping.
I don't understand,
my knees don't bend well.
Babies don't sweat and I'm no baby.
Why don't they move from the blood? Blank
and twitching as shot deer, they look
to me. They didn't mean it, but someone is dead.
Now, I'm telling myself, time to wake up,
I don't have to be here, I know I'm not three.
No playing 'cause knives hurt.
I have to find a hiding
place for it, this secret
is for a crack to eat.
But shh, don't worry, go!
The blade gestures in my hand
for my parents to run.

George Leong

I was born in October of 1950 in San Francisco's Chinatown. My published works are included in my book, A lone Bamboo doesn't come from Jackson Street *(1977) Isthmus Press, and various anthologies including* Califia, Yardbird, Time to Greez, AION, Texas Long Grain *and* American Born and Foreign. *I also have a work in a Japan anthology* Ode to Bill Sorro. *I am currently completing a novel and struggling to start another. For money, I work as a freelance video operator and in sound. I have also received an Artists in the Communities grant in 1976 to run the Asian American Writers' Workshop in San Francisco with the Kearny Street Workshop, a Chinatown community arts organization. I co-founded the writers' workshop with Al Robles.*

This is Our Music

This is our music
latinos chinos africas
the clef of Asian America
an American sound

This is our music
unfiltered/natural
transbiotic/soul jump
slapping fingers
of congeros canton
play koto with mbira fingers

This is our music
by way of the greed
of European castaways
over a nation of refugees
slaves
those lost souls
our kidnapped wrists
bound
can you imagine
Adolf Sax rolling in his grave
to John Coltrane
    Gerald Oshita
    Gato
    Baba
would a stradivarius dream
be Mark Izu
    Ray Brown
    Jason Huang
    Leroy Jenkins

Soul Food!
We are a nation of ghost chains
pulling a world of mostly color
whose overseer try to bind us
from our love songs
        prison songs
Soul Food!
the drone melodies of the plains indian
the hopi
whose footsteps could have trekked the Bering Straits
trickling thunder for a living
going on forever
Soul Food!
listen to the lion's roar
the ancient route between Asia and Africa
the vomit
and the smell of death
in the boats that brought us here
the chorus of

a thousand Chinatowns
all the way to Mississippi
the latin woks of cocinas chinas
the scratches of homemade chisels
etching history on Angel Island walls
polyrhythmic melodies of children's cries

This is our music
that latin chinas africas
an american sound
unfiltered
and going on forever

a sometimes love poem

At one time
we ate our rice
together
two grains at a time/ made
counterbeats of slow chews
made nourishment
so honest
romance in our swallows

but at night
you steal the fields
you burn them in my sleep
the charred root
so young
haven't ever learned to cry
your false mountains
would cast no shadows
your oceans
startle mirages
and your sand
would laugh like broken glass
and our lovemaking
becomes vinegared wine
cupped with bare scarred shivering hands
and your love
sullen morbid
as if you were trying to tell me
I should have learned
what I was born to do

to eat my rice alone

Walter Lew

Born in Baltimore, 1955, to two doctors fresh from Korea—one dreamy, the other, with both parents gone, still full of the old colonial curse. (Colonial Chōsen (1909-45): one of the rice and labor farms for Japan's "Greater East Asian Co-prosperity Sphere"; end of 2000 years of Korean kings; Mitsubishi et al take over, climax in 30,000 Korean deaths at Hiroshima.) Grew up in "Bawl'mer" on the Orioles (era of the Robinson Boys, Boog, and Mike Cuellar's screwball), "The Wasteland" constantly intoned in backseats, 1960's suicide and neurosis poets, Sgt. Pepper, McCoy Tyner, and the French Symbolism, Stevens, and Schönberg/Berg/Webern of two psychedelic friends. Father showed me war and "High Noon"; Mother modernist painting and Hollywood actresses. Barely perceived 1968 but almost got killed anyway. In college, loss of Keatsian "negative capability" led to hiding out in cool sciences, A's for med school, but bolted back to poesy when the time to enlist came. But "The road back to 詩 is hard, phiu! phiu! . . ." Wittgensteinian depression, thin Orientalism: no true yūgen; stupefied by a certain death, consequent guilt and grayed

151

matter. "*So we cut our hair / And made lower class money / And were surprised to find nothing / In being un-rare...*" Thought grad school would save me; dusty, unmotivated, childish *(separation of systems from what...)* Confusion in Tokyo. "*The road to* 詩 *is hard, harder than climbing blue heaven.*" In New York, assistant editor of NUCLEAR TIMES, poetry editor of BRIDGE—please send poems! Performed and conceiving of new mediums for poetry *(e.g. last year's* benshi/pyŏnsa *performances for Renee Tajima's Asian American Film Festival: poetry and music accompanying silent films).* Would bet on Video X Poetry; therefore, Nam June Paik's "Allen's Complaint" will be seen as seminal. Boku no hosomichi. *Kim Sŭng-ok: "Long ago, there was once a youth who got a bad palm reading. Afterwards, he worked hard at trying to cut good lines into his palms.*"

Leaving Seoul: 1953

We have to bury the urns,
Mother and I. We tried to leave them in a back room,
Decoyed by a gas lamp, and run out

But they landed behind us here, at the front gate.
It is 6th hour, early winter, black cold:
Only, on the other side of the rice-paper doors

The yellow *ondol* stone-heated floors
Are still warm. I look out to the blue
Lanterns along the runway, the bright airplane.

Off the back step, Mother, disorganized
As usual, has devised a clumsy rope and pulley
To bury the urns. I wonder out loud

How she ever became a doctor.
Get out, she says *Go to your father: he too
Does not realize what is happening.* You see,

Father is waiting at the airfield in a discarded U.S. Army
Overcoat. He has lost his hat, lost
His father, and is smoking Lucky's like crazy ...

We grab through the tall weeds and wind
That begin to shoot under us like river ice.
It is snowing. We are crying, from the cold

Or what? It is only decades
Later that, tapping the tall glowing jars,
I find they contain all that has made
The father have dominion over hers.

Urn I: Silent for Twenty-Five Years,
The Father of My Mother Advises Me (Excerpts)

Careless
but not fearless

You spin out for the great cities:
hang-outs, libraries
heavy-boned churches
you never knew the magic of

Subway troubadors
taxicab Orphées
Dump you wind-stroked in the larynx
of alley after alley, contemplating

Light petaling through fire escapes
like your own seasons, like the one
long season you hesitate
to dig up and divine: Ours, and not of those

Leaping by in the snow-lit mouth
behind you, beyond the dumpster
To swirl down numbered Aves
with the cars and commerce

Everything with its colors
on, everything marked to leave your
Own 詩 heart, own mouth magic
SHI
gabbing to a brick

*

As you sprint away from me
your black hair lengthens,
bounds, like the billowing, squid-
dyed flame of ocean

I once saw unfurl across
a kabuki stage when I was
a foreign student of law
at a Tokyo university.

Tied to my bones
your hair is taut,
twists in the riven
spewing hole of mud

Above me, and as the sky and moon
run right to the edge
of the hills around
my grave, and you chase

The melon light down
the far faces,
your scalp's sinews
rear and gasp: Resound

before they snap,
snarl through the dust
collapsing behind you: tendon, weeds,
lizard, pod snagged

In the lash at the end
Of each resinous strand.
Here, in the mound
I hold on to my end.

III.

Leaving the ginseng-rocked mountain pass
South of Ch'ung-ju,
Go up the dust road,
Across the reservoir, along

The muddy ridges of the toad-sung
Paddies, past the farmer-gravekeeper's house.
Tell his children rinsing
Melons at the pump you'll stop in later;
Even if he comes out then, do not pause
For *makkoli* or chatter.

At the burial slope's gate
The road ends like an uplifted tongue.
With your touch if not in characters
Read the omphalos there, and climb up

And bow down three times before each living
Nourishing wild-haired mound,
Before each of the thirty-two generations:
And know clearly, grandson,

Our reply
By the song of the crickets there.

(. . .)

Fan

for Rick Rohdenberg

I used to believe I wouldn't live past 16:
That was Norm Siebern's number
And he seemed to me the epitome
    of minor, unspoken tragedy.
Stolid, St. Louis-German, crew-cut lefty with
Specs who hit a bunch of homers
And .290 for the Stengel Yankees, he blew
A Series game by dropping an easy fly
And was unloaded young on the Orioles, converted into
A 1st baseman and hit nothing for a few dull summers
Before fading from the field—without a press conference or
    final trot around the bases.
I wanted to Norm Siebern's son,
I wanted a father who could chaw Red Chief
And know how to shut up and leave things alone
While Baltimore won a pennant without him.
I knew Norm would never reach the Sunday averages or 20
Homers again, yet whenever I was at the stadium
I would scream for him to be put in:
He still had that golden, Yankee lefty
Stroke—though too slow now—
And had resigned himself to pinch-hitting with the calm
Of a Chūshingura rōnin.
(Once he even led the league in walks, i.e.
    in patience.)
Whenever he hit into a double play
(He was almost as slow as Killebrew)
I would get so depressed that
It was impossible to do anymore homework that night
For Mr. Axe, Miss Washing-machine, or
Miss Bitter... Norm,
        Dad,
One afternoon we were playing a doubleheader against the Angels
I had a box with that brat Jay DeMarco and his father
Right behind 3rd base and kept screaming at Bauer
    to put you in.
He didn't, but in the middle of the 5th of the last game
You stared at me like an ostrich over top of the dugout,
Disappeared, then rose like Boog Powell or Hondo Howard
(I never dreamed you were so big!) and gave me
Silently, nodding
One of your own
Cracked bats, your name
Looped into the fat, ash barrel.
That shut me up for a while... Norm,
Do you remember? No washed-up .240 choke was ever rooted for
As you were by me—none of my friends
Could fathom it, but
Can you root
        for *me* now?

I'm writing this so I won't kill myself
I never thought I'd get past your number
But here I am, still fanning, still
Fouling everything off. I think it's because I never
Had a good year with the Yankees
And therefore can't go out with grace,
Personal honor or be stoical about the stats...
Is that it?
O, Silent batsman kneeling lonely
In the dark outfields of obscurity!
All night I've been shaking the old bat
Searching its fault for your secret.

Two Handfuls of *Waka* for
Thelonious Sphere Monk (d. Feb. 1982)

When Monk laid it down
Each note would blur a moment and
Pass on: pure, midnight.

Cut into time like ruby:
In the hard, celestial chord.

            *

Passed on pure, midnight:
Now they tune the stars like sharps,
Jar the dark alive

And the cold space carves his song
Till it pierces the other world

            *

Jars the dark. Alive?
A priest did say "He is
Received into bliss

    Eternal—jamming with God's best
    in that Great hymn of Praise. . ."

True, he is freed from
Misery of this or that.
But also things like

    Green chimneys, Off minors and
    Billie Holiday in red

Can no more wander
In his stride, slide and wangle. . .
Close to the end of

    the world anyway: What difference a
    Misterioso or Epistrophy?

            *

Still, when in the quartz
Chapel, strong Randy Weston
Raised Monk's song, hundreds

    In their midtown scramble paused,
    Seraphing the high windows

Galleries, aisles,
And crowded the pulpit, budged
The altar. It was

    Not you and yet your time in
    Randy's hands did illumine each

Mind. We knew your Song
Not heaven, was the great sphere
And that it was for us

    to play it at our best—
    Received now into Thelonious,

I Mean You, into
Humph and Introspection: their key
Eternal bliss

    Though it is only now,
    Near the end of the world

      *

That we might pass on
What he taught us to hear: the silent
Trembling inside

    Each beat; the distance between
    The Raised 1 and Flat 2:

Ourselves and Ourselves.
As Monk laid it down and
Passed on: pure, round

    Midnight

Photo by Shulee Ong

Genny Lim

Genny Lim is the author of the award winning play, PAPER ANGELS,
co-author of ISLAND: Poetry and History of Chinese Immigrants on Angel
Island, 1910-1940 *(Hoc-Doi, 1980), and author of the children's book,*
WINGS FOR LAI HO, *(East/West Pub. Co., 1982).*

*Ms. Lim is also the founder of PAPER ANGELS PRODUCTIONS, a
theater arts organization located in San Francisco Chinatown. She is the
mother of two daughters, ages six and one years and teaches Creative
Writing at UC Berkeley's Asian American Studies Department.*

Visiting Father

Backtracking
Fifty miles past Bakersfield
Watching the road fork
like a bloodhound sniffing out
your father's grave

Empty-handed with
no flowers, no tears to
hide the shame
Bridging the 23-year silence
with filial apologies

Inside the car waiting
my bones hollow
I watch a figure weave in and out
rows of moonlit gravestones
pointing out, naming each ghost with
a rain-choked voice
Aunt Alice here, father over there ...
The little girl holding your hand
Mute to the strange rumbling of demons
inside you

Departure

Please tell me how you are not afraid
While I cover your shoulders, big sister
I'll pretend it's morning and
the fog has lifted

Please open your eyes
Let me hear you yawn like a child
Let me see your smile
Talk about the old days
in your Chinatown accent

If there is an odor of stale incense
withered roses mingled with antiseptic spray
You can criticize my house-cleaning
I won't mind
if you scold
the way you did when I borrowed
your white satin cheongsam without asking
and spilled sweet and sour sauce on it
fifteen years ago

I won't avoid your eyes
staring out of their sockets like glass
When I ask how you are
I won't hear you choking
When I rise to leave you
I won't notice your hands trembling
reaching for me
from your bed
across the TV tray
fumbling with cotton gauze, syringe
3 cc's of morphine
shot thru your brain

I won't flinch
I won't cry

Sweet 'n Sour

Buy a fresh chicken
Boil in the pot till tender
Siu Kum, sixth daughter
Cook the jai
w/ ample oysters 'n black mushrooms

I have a husband who yells
a baby who cries
I have not looked in a mirror
for fear of seeing the future

Sometimes
I sit by the window
when everyone sleeps
Night encloses me
in the fold of her lap
Once again I become Ma-ku
Sorceress of the Underdog
Reclaimer of the Sea

Gung Hay Fat Choy
Find a nice Chinese boy
Get married, make kids
A son to carry on your husband's name
Serve tea to in-laws
Be happy, after all
you might have been an old maid

A ripe pomelo on the mantel is
a symbol of fertility
The Chinese know all about
Sweet 'n sour

Wonder Woman

Sometimes I see reflections on bits of glass on sidewalks
I catch the glimmer of empty bottles floating out to sea
Sometimes I stretch my arms way above my head and wonder if
There are women along the Mekong doing the same

Sometimes I stare longingly at women who I will never know
Generous, laughing women with wrinkled cheeks and white teeth
Dragging along chubby, rosy-cheeked babies on fat, wobbly legs
Sometimes I stare at Chinese grandmothers
Getting on the 30 Stockton with shopping bags
Japanese women tourists in European hats
Middle-aged mothers with laundry carts
Young wives holding hands with their husbands
Lesbian women holding hands in coffee-houses
Smiling debutantes with bouquets of yellow daffodils
Silver-haired matrons with silver rhinestoned poodles
Painted prostitutes posing along MacArthur Boulevard
Giddy teenage girls snapping gum in fast cars
Widows clutching bibles, crucifixes

I look at them and wonder if
They are a part of me
I look in their eyes and wonder if
They share my dreams

I wonder if the woman in mink is content
if the stockbroker's wife is afraid of growing old
If the professor's wife is an alcoholic
If the woman in prison is me

There are copper-tanned women in Hyannis Port playing tennis
Women who eat with finger bowls
There are women in factories punching time clocks
Women tired every waking hour of the day

I wonder why there are women born with silver spoons
      in their mouths
Women who have never known a day of hunger
Women who have never changed their own bed linen
And I wonder why there are women who must work
Women who must clean other women's houses
Women who must shell shrimps for pennies a day
Women who must sew other women's clothes
Who must cook
Who must die
In childbirth
In dreams

Why must a woman stand divided?
Building the walls that tear them down?
Jill-of-all-trades
Lover, mother, housewife, friend, breadwinner
Heart and spade
A woman is a ritual
A house that must accommodate
A house that must endure
Generation after generation
Of wind and torment, of fire and rain
A house with echoing rooms
Closets with hidden cries
Walls with stretchmarks
Windows with eyes

Short, tall, skinny, fat
Pregnant, married, white, yellow, black, brown, red
Professional, working-class, aristocrat
Women cooking over coals in sampans
Women shining tiffany spoons in glass houses
Women stretching their arms way above the clouds
In Samarkand, in San Francisco
Along the Mekong

Stephen Shu Ning Liu

Stephen Shu Ning Liu was born in Fu Ling (16 March 1930), China, son of a hermitic painter of waterlilies. A poet himself, his mandarin-scholar grandfather taught him Chinese classics. At the age of 10 Liu shocked his parents by announcing his passion to be a soldier or a sailor. And by a twist of fate he almost became his own prophet when he joined an expeditionary army in World War II. Later, he attended Nanking University and found his studies in Chinese boring; without his parents' consent he sailed for Taiwan where he taught Chinese for a year, and then he left China for San Francisco in 1952.

While studying in America, he worked on odd jobs: once a dishwasher, a hamburger cook, a white mice caretaker and a janitor. After decades of struggle he has published more than 200 poems in English, has earned several academic degrees including a Ph.D. in English from the University of North Dakota. He has taught English at Northern Montana College, College of San Mateo, and since 1973 he has been teaching at Clark County Community College, Las Vegas, Nevada.

For the New World Press *(Beijing, China) Liu has himself translated his English poems into Chinese; and* Dream Journeys to China, *in bilingual format, his first full-length collection of poems, appeared in 1982. He was awarded the 1982 Creative Writing Fellowship Grant from the National Endowment for the Arts.*

   My philosophy in writing poetry is that poetic language should be simple, clear and direct. Like fresh air and wholesome bread, poetry is for the crowd; and the poet, since he is just another human being, does not necessarily have a tattoo or a weird hairdo. A poet should work alone and leave group exercise to the football players.
   The roots of poetry will grow stronger in the soil of poverty or sorrow. Shakespeare's words, "Sweet are the uses of adversity," depict best the birth of poetry. The song of a nightingale is therefore for the poet.
   Good poems are fewer than morning stars. No serious poet should publish more than two or three volumes of poetry in his/her lifetime. Let's face the fact: how many passages or sonnets from Shakespeare (or any other great poet) will survive "the slow-chapped power" of time, less than 20 pages perhaps?

My Father's Martial Art

When he came home Mother said he looked
like a monk and stank of green fungus.
At the fireside he told us about life
at the monastery: his rock pillow,
his cold bath, his steel-bar lifting
and his wood-chopping. He didn't see
a woman for three winters, on Mountain O Mei.

"My Master was both light and heavy.
He skipped over treetops like a squirrel.
Once he stood on a chair, one foot tied
to a rope. We four pulled; we couldn't
move him a bit. His kicks could split
a cedar's trunk."

I saw Father break into a pumpkin
with his fingers. I saw him drop a hawk
with bamboo arrows. He rose before dawn, filled
our backyard with a harsh sound *hah, hah, hah*:
there was his Black Dragon Sweep, his Crane Stand,
his Mantis Walk, his Tiger Leap, his Cobra Coil ...
Infrequently he taught me tricks and made me
fight the best of all the village boys.

From a busy street I brood over high cliffs
on O Mei, where my father and his Master sit:
shadows spread across their faces as the smog
between us deepens into a funeral pyre.

But don't retreat into night, my father.
Come down from the cliffs. Come
with a single Black Dragon Sweep and hush
this oncoming traffic with your *hah, hah, hah.*

I Lie on the Chilled Stones of The Great Wall

A northwind dies half way to the Gobi Desert,
as I lie on the chilled stones of the Wall:
watch towers sway above me like steel helmets,
sunlight of Chin Dynasty fades into lamp beams
at farm windows, unknown seasons fall in ashes,
white-headed mothers lament over the snow;
Emperor Chin must have one hundred mountains removed.

My naked arms glue to the ancient fort,
my ears listen to the far-off bugles.
I see Su Wu moving with his herd, by the North Sea,
19-year captivity, tears freezing in his old face.
"Nay, you may not return," the savage Chief says;
"unless your male sheep have become pregnant . . ."
I see Zao Cheun's sedan in a blizzard, her beauty
once shining through Ch'ang Ann streets, her heart
forever longing for a home, per Pi Pa and her song
saddening the air at the foreign court; and before
the skies of West Han turning dark, over the ridges

more barbarian arrows come down like locusts,
but the Mid-Kingdom's banners stand; riders march on:
lances clashing, shields colliding. Kill, kill, kill!
Invaders wince and scamper about like frightening mice,
battle cries of Li Ling's braves shake up the earth,
their bright swords have smashed a thousand warriors
of Fu, and the clouds over my head amass in wild beasts.

I find myself staggering among the fallen chariots,
bumping into the manes and breath of dying horses;
in the struggle I've been wrestling with something
grizzly, whose eyes are glinting like flames, whose icy
paws sinking deep into my flesh. I endure the pain, and
with my scimitar I cut his swinish mouth open. The taste
of blood nauseates me. I wake to the chattering tourists:
the 1975 midsummer sun shines on me like an illusion,
two thousand years swirling through my bones at once.

Adultery at a Las Vegas Bookstore

after T. S. ELIOT

Let's go, you and I,
rambling through the casinos of gray-
yellow smog on a sweaty summer's day,
& after some oysters at a sound-and-fury
cabaret & a few hours in a cheap motel,
let's water Waller's lovely rose in deserts
of vast eternity, let's pass Troy's last wall,
see Helen in her tears & in her unbound hair,
let's come by la fenetre en mansarde where Emma
rises from her death-bed, in the mad singing of
that blind beggar, & down some windy shoreline
off Viareggio, let's gather together Shelley's
wave-torn poems, let's cover Byron's fever-
corroded bones in Missolonghi's grass, & since

Las Vegas sun looks hostile, let's go, you and I,
cheek to cheek, our fingers entwined, let's go
sauntering, moon-shod, with Frieda Lawrence, &
before the roosters crow, let's go climbing the
Elsinore, let's hear the Ghost roaring below the
cold terrace, "Swear! O Hamlet, swear!"

On Pali Lookout

I was easy, a somnambulist, as I climbed
ladders into the sky, into a water-color painting
that had amused me on a brick wall.
But the Tourist Guide's voice wakes me:
"Three hundred tribe warriors leaped
to their death from this cliff. No one surrendered.
You hear the ghosts in the wind, wind, wind."
True, we can't stand firm on the stone parapet
this evening. Bamboo groves on the mountaintops
bend over like disheveled women. Clouds threaten
the shorelines with driven horses, funeral banners.

Darkly gleaming, Honolulu sprawls eastward
and diminishes into terraced paddies in mist.
Can anyone here recall that hermit-painter
on river Yangtze? He never painted a seascape
fierce like this. His brushes breathed quiet life
of a pagoda, a heron hidden in reeds, a lotus pond
by maple woods, a fisherman in his straw frock,
or a late sampan homing under a flaming sky.
He chanted transcendental verses by glass windows.
His hand quickened in mild September light.

Now his ancient eyes stare at me
through the haze. His voice vibrates the air:
"While the mountain rain hastens this way,
the wind beats hard against our balcony.
Evil auguries seize our nation: earth trembles,
locusts waste the land. Civil strife must come."

And he was his own prophet. Flood rushed
in that winter, and then a red-eye hurricane
from Siberia. His balcony crumbled; his body
couldn't be found after the Revolution until

this hour a blast from the Pacific chills me,
bringing back the same smell on river Yangtze
and the same portentous voice that cries out
for thirty years in my blood:
"While the mountain rain hastens this way,
the wind beats hard against our balcony . . ."

Honolulu slumps into the evening mist.
The sea-cliff quivers, tips over and shadows me
like the missed corpse in the village:
the whirlwind that blew us apart pushes us
together on Pali Lookout, father and son.

A Pair of Fireflies

After a heart disease, Aunt Li died;
her face turned white, lily in windless pond.

The kerosene lamp under her feet,
the country Priest said, might light her
path to a land of tortuous tunnels.

The blood dripping through her left nostril,
we believed, was a sign
of her Sixth Sense.

Aunt Li gave me a bear hug, almost
suffocating me, whenever she caught me
running around the house;

and we chased after fireflies in the woods:
being fat, Aunt Li couldn't go fast.
She called me, out of breath:

"Wait, little monkey. Quit that running!
I've a pair of fireflies for you. Get your
glass jar. Quit that running, little monkey."

For three decades her laughing voice pricks
my ear, her false teeth gleam, her lamp burns
under her protruding feet, and by some

hillside, darker than night,
her eyes blink, tirelessly winking.

Wing Tek Lum

Honolulu, Hawaii
It is my strong preference not to have a photo, statement, etc. Let the poems speak for themselves.

The Poet Imagines
His Grandfather's Thoughts on the Day He Died

This is the first year
the Dragon Eyes tree has ever borne fruit:
let us see what this omen brings.
Atop one of its exposed roots
a small frog squats, not moving, not even blinking.
I remember when my children were young
and this whole front yard was a taro patch:
we would take them out at night with a lantern
blinding the frogs just long enough
to sneak a hook up under the belly.
In those days we grew taro
as far as the eye could see;
I even invented a new kind of trough
lined inside with a wire mesh
so we could peel the skins with ease.
The King bought our poi,
and gave me a pounder one day.
It is made of stone,
and looks like the clapper of a bell, smooth and heavy.
I keep it in my bedroom now—there—on the dresser.
The fish we call Big Eyes
lies on an oval plate beside it.
I have not been hungry today.
The full bowl of rice attracts a fly
buzzing in anticipation.
I hear the laughter of one of my grandchildren
from the next room: which one is it?
Maybe someday one of them will think of me
and see the rainbows that I have seen,
the opium den in Annam that frightened me so,
my mother's tears when I left home.

Dear ancestors, all this is still one in my mind.

Translations

for Jeffery Paul Chan
in appreciation for his letter
to the editor, New York Review
of Books, *April 28, 1977*

1

Ghosts: they conjure
up childhood
scenes—me running around in
old bedsheets, reading
about Caspar
next to a comic
rack, marvelling at
the trick
camerawork for Cosmo G. Topper.

Gwai: I am older now,
sometimes catch previews
to those Shaw Brothers horror
films, at the
library research ancient
rites of exorcism for
the baneful
who brought pestilence and
drought. There are also,
I have
learned, Old Demons who wear
white skin
and make believe
they behave
like men.

2

The Chinaman gave
the Demon what
the former thought
the latter thought
were things
Chinese: a comedy
of errors,
part fawning, part
deception and contempt.
There is no
word for
fortune cookie in Cantonese.

3

Tòhng Yàhn Gāai was what
we once called
where we
lived: "China-People-
Street." Later, we mimicked
Demon talk
and wrote down only
Wàh Fauh—"China-Town."
The difference
is obvious: the people
disappeared.

Chinatown Games

inspired by Fung Shiu-Ying's
Chinese Children's Games *(ARTS,
Inc., New York City, 1972)*

1. Choosing Sides

Little girls
on the sidewalk
chanting in a circle
an even number of them
each offering
a hand outstretched
some palms up
some down.
When by chance
an equal number
show up as down
they gather their teams
ready to play
no hint of ability
just the fun of the game.

2. Sugar Stuck Beans

An even number of kids:
one of them It.
Safety is found
in sticking together—
a pair of beans.
The It can tag you
only if you're alone.
The little ones scream
weave about parked cars
arms locked.
Some sacrifice security
gladly breaking a pair
to distract the It
saving another
dodging all by himself.

3. Hawk Grabbing Chicks

Arms waving
the mother hen
holds her ground
in front of the hawk
her children undulating
in a single line
behind her.
The hawk must go around
to snatch any stray
who might let go
as the hen angles
towards the hydrant
her noisy brood
hands to waist clinging on
for dear life.

To the Old Masters

"They may have left behind an honored name
But it cost a lifetime of deprivation."
    —*T'ao Ch'ien*

I have no wife,
much less a son, to lament over
when he has died
in his infancy. I have never
seen a peach
blossom in the bud,
nor stood beneath
the Red Cliffs awed by
their towering history. Alcohol
tastes bitter
to me; I have always shunned
such classic delights.
Few friends
of mine write
poems—even letters are hard to
compose: how can we
swap our sentiments? Pouring
over your lyrics,
the translations at my
side, I worry about how
muddle-headed my past innocence
has made me. This
is my only
claim to sorrow. Whatever
glimpses I have
caught of the vision within
your words must be due to
your daring: as
the moon on this night
illumines to the far reaches
of my room,
beaming through a window
cluttered now with
clothes, drying in the breeze.

                    Quarry Bay, 1974

176

At a Chinaman's Grave

*"Kingston, too, looked critically at
it ('Chinaman') as not being meaning-
ful for her ... She said she even tried
'Chinaperson' and 'Chinawoman' and
found they didn't work either, the
first sounding 'terrible' and the
second being inaccurate."*

(The Honolulu Advertiser, 6/22/78)

My grandmother's
brother here
died all alone, wife
and children back
in the village. He
answered to
"Chinaman" like all
the others
of our race back then.
The Demons hired
only lonely
men, not their
sweethearts,
taai pòh, baby
daughters. They laid
ties, cut cane, but
could not proliferate. They took
on woman's
work, by default,
washing shirts,
frying eggs and sausages.
Granduncle cooked.
From what he earned
he sent
money home,
gambled perhaps, maybe hid
some away—all for
one purpose. Those old men:
they lived
their whole
lives with souls
somewhere else, their hearts
burdened of
hopes, waiting to
be reunited.
Some succeeded
and we
are the fruits of those
reunions. Some
did not,
and they are
now forgotten, but for
these tombstones,
by the rest.

Laureen Mar

Laureen Mar was born in Seattle, Washington in 1953. She has lived six years in New York City. Her chapbook Living Furniture *was published in 1982. Most recently, her work has been published in Macmillan's* Women Poets of the World. *She is one of the editors of* Asian American Poets—North and South, Contact II publications. *She leaves New York City to return to Seattle to write fiction, full-time.*

Black Rocks

1.

Your mother poses on black rocks.
The sun flares white behind her.
Is it the sun that makes her dark eyes frown
this time—the camera, or the child
who waits to lean against her skirt,
the yellow jungle that promises
heat and a torrid wind?

2.

You were born on black rocks.
You climbed the jagged
face against your mother's
warning, digging your way past yellow
and white daisies, the frail iris.
From the neighbor you stole whatever
was in season, crabapples, cherries.

3.

You fall against black rocks.
The sky opens, startled
green leaves rising above you faster
than your hands. You lie in the grass
listening to your mother rushing,
your lips bleeding brightly.
Your mouth shows a faint bone-white scar.

At Wonder Donut

— Chinatown, San Francisco

My mother whispers to my father
"that's her, sitting there"—
the lady grandpa married over here.
She looks younger than my grandma.
She has two children with her, too.
My father orders donuts,
gold puffs sprinkled with white sugar,
the insides like carved ivory balls,
one tumbling in another.
I eat them hot and watch the old lady
by the kitchen wrap wonton.
The skin flat in one hand,
a silver knife in the other
swiping meat from a bowl, slap
on the skin, water on the knife,
slap! skin! twist! throw! She tosses
wonton over her wrinkled head
like a circus juggler.
She could be blind!
My father smiles at my staring
and asks if I have enough donuts to eat.
I smile and hold up my hands.
I can hear the wonton whispering,
sinking into the bucket,
their newborn eyes pale and soft.

The Immigration Act of 1924

I've taken the police squad outline from where you fell,
you remember, years ago, you heaved yourself up on the
      window ledge
of a rundown hotel and jumped?   Well, they traced you
      on the sidewalk
in chalk.   The figure vaguely resembled you, a little
      amorphous
and anonymous, the way they liked you.

              I peeled you off the sidewalk as carefully
              as I could,
making sure you had all your fingers; brought you home,
and propped you up like a cardboard doll.

                  Now you'll do
                      as I say.
Sit here in this chair by the window.   I'll let you look out
if you promise to behave.   Behave!

               Are you thinking
about your wife?   She's been stranded years in China,
feeding the chickens and ducks.   You didn't know
a beautiful country could keep her out?

              Don't tell me
you're not accustomed.   You've done well, the railroads—
don't shake your head like that!   I tell you, I learned
about the railroads in school, listen!—you must do as I say.
Sit here by the window and fold clothes.

                Yes, fold clothes.
Later we'll go outside and feed the pigeons together.   Look,
don't you see, for you I've painted this room gray?   Sit
      here
and fold your trousers and shirts, over and over, yes,
      there are
no other colors in your closet.   Only gray, like moths,
      like spit,
like this battered tin pot.   You won't go crazy, there are
      plenty
of men like you for you to drink tea with.

                Get down off the
                window!

Get down, and fold these clothes, the same worn trousers
      and shirts.
Yes, like that, smooth the creases, they'll leave a fine,
sharp line.   Yes, keep folding clothes, I'll shake them out
for you to fold again, I'll bring you more men's clothes,
just keep folding them and folding them until you learn
you can't just die and take yourself away.

The Window Frames the Moon

Some nights the moon is the curve of a comb,
tumble of night held casually;
other nights, a plate broken perfectly in half,
box of night coveting the smooth edge.

The window frames the moon, places it
to the left of the world, to the right,
decides if it floats, hurtles, suspends,
glances, antagonizes, surrenders.

By eleven the moon is as certain and fixed
as the clock on the dresser,
the chink in the wall,
the black tablecloth with silver dots of glitter.

Every night is the opportunity to rearrange the world!
With the window, I push the moon into place
as if it were a vase of flowers.
Oh, the glory of the night contained!

But there are nights the moon looms large,
so large it refuses to fit in the frame,
so large it refuses to splinter,
and when I push the moon, it pushes back

and fills my house, and I am forced to abandon
the clock and the dresser
to stand with the trees, leaves, grass,
taking my place among the small things of the world.

Photo by George Dean

Diane Mei Lin Mark

* *From Hawaii. Now dividing her time between Hawaii and New York*
* *B.A., English and Asian Studies, Mills College, Oakland, California*
* *M.A., American Studies, University of Hawaii*
* *Travelled and lived in Asia as a scholarship grantee of the East-West Center Communication Institute*
* *Studied filmmaking at New York University*
* *Has worked as a newspaper reporter; oral history researcher; writer/ associate producer for PEARLS, a documentary film series on Asian Americans aired nationally on PBS*
* *Articles and poetry have appeared in publications such as* Bulletin for Concerned Asian Scholars, Sino-American Relations, Asian Women, Third World Women, Impulse, Asian Americans in Hawaii
* *Project Director/Writer, A Place Called Chinese America, a history of Chinese in the U.S., published by Kendall/Hunt in 1982*
* *Currently developing new book and film projects*

Rice and Rose Bowl Blues

I remember the day
Mama called me in from
the football game with brothers
and neighbor boys
in our front yard

said it was time
I learned to
wash rice for dinner

glancing out the window
I watched a pass interception
setting the other team up
on our 20

> *Pour some water
> into the pot,*
> she said pleasantly,
> turning on the tap
> *Rub the rice
> between your hands,
> pour out the clouds,
> fill it again*
> (I secretly traced
> an end run through
> the grains in
> between pourings)

with the rice
settled into a simmer
I started out the door
but was called back

the next day
Roland from across the street
sneeringly said he heard
I couldn't play football
anymore

I laughed loudly,
asking him
where
he'd heard
such a thing

Liberation

this revelation, the retreat of tide
from our shore,
slowly peeling back ocean's edge
unveiling a new world of
men and women
throwing out memorized lines
running to each other in slow motion
ringing pure
like the temple bell at twilight

we face each other
in bare knowing, blue wind
over the Pali
shooting into our veins

at dusk
expanding circles touch
and we speak
a wordless language

in dress rehearsal
night after night
I dream the revelation,
the retreat of tide from shore

And The Old Folks Said

and the old folks said
my face must always
be as calm as
a still mountain lake filled
with the moon's reflections

   I say there's
   no turning back—

     they shoot rapids
     in America!

the cry is
welling up inside me
and
that all/night moon
will soon be
pieces of light
. floating
   down
     stream

Kula ... A Homecoming

it was my first

time in Kula
but i felt as if
i had come home

old country roads lined
with keawe trees. round
mountains yellow and
dry to dark timber line.
Chang's General Store
and Maui potato chips and
schoolhouse where Popo
taught now empty and cool
in shade of elephant trees

after sugar plantations
they settled on rocky slopes
of Haleakala volcano. tilled
untillable soil. gave the
land a facelift

planted irish potatoes for
California gold miners.
fields of young corn. yard
greens to tsao and brew soup.
rice and ham tsoi steaming
continually in evening oven

85 Hakka families
struggled here from the
1840s and then
took ships to Honolulu
where the day was not as endless

but when the harvest was good
in the early years, a luau.
panini booze. huli huli pig.
poi. lomi salmon. and rice.
native Hawaiians came to
serenade at Chinese New Year
and in December they made
Christmas trees with ferns

over the door
of the meeting hall
a character inscription
carved during the
drought of 1905:
"United in strength."

Suzie Wong Doesn't Live Here

Suzie Wong
doesn't live here anymore
yeah, and
Madame Butterfly
and the geisha ladies have all
gone
to
lunch (hey, they might
    be gone a very
    long
    time)

no one here
but
ourselves

       stepping on,
without downcast eyes,
without calculating dragon power,
without tight red cheongsams
  embroidered with peonies
without the
silence
that you've come to
know so well
and we,
to feel so alien with

seeing each other at last
so little needs to be explained

there is this strength

born female in Asian America,
our dreams stored years
in the backrooms
of our minds

now happening—
like sounds of flowers
bathed in noontime light
reaching righteously skyward!

Janice Mirikitani

Janice Mirikitani, third-generation Japanese American, is a poet, choreographer, teacher and community organizer. She is Program Director of Glide Church/Urban Center, a multi-racial and multi-cultural institution in San Francisco known for its social activism. As part of her responsibilities, she has created and directs an arts program that includes theater, dance, poetry, writing and music.

In her work as a poet and editor for the past 15 years, Janice Mirikitani has been an editor for a number of anthologies, including Aion magazine, Third World Women, Time to Greez! Incantations from the Third World. Her most recent accomplishment is the publication of AYUMI, A Japanese American Anthology, for which she served as Project Director and Editor. AYUMI, a 320-page bi-lingual anthology, features four generations of Japanese-American writers, poets and graphic artists.

Janice Mirikitani's poetry and short fiction is collected in her book, Awake in the River (Isthmus Press, San Francisco). She has been published in many anthologies, textbooks and magazines, including Asian American Heritage, The Ethnic American Woman, American Born and Foreign, The Third World Woman: Minority Women Writers in the U.S., Amerasia Journal and Bridge magazine, to name a few.

Breaking Silence

For my mother's testimony
before Commission on Wartime Relocation and
Internment of Japanese American Civilians

There are miracles that happen
she said.
From the silences
in the glass caves of our ears,
from the crippled tongue,
from the mute, wet eyelash,
testimonies waiting like winter.
　　We were told
that silence was better
golden like our skin,
　　useful like
go quietly,
　　easier like
don't make waves,
　　expedient like
horsetails and deserts.

　　　　　　　　　　　"Mr. Commissioner ...
　　　　　　　　　　　... the U.S. Army Signal Corps confiscated
　　　　　　　　　　　our property ... it was subjected to vandalism
　　　　　　　　　　　and ravage.　All improvements we had made
　　　　　　　　　　　before our incarceration was stolen
　　　　　　　　　　　or destroyed ...
　　　　　　　　　　　I was coerced into signing documents
　　　　　　　　　　　giving you authority to take ..."
　　　　　　　　　　　... to take
　　　　　　　　　　　... to take.

My mother,
soft like tallow,
words peeling from her
like slivers
of yellow flame,
her testimony
a vat of boiling water
surging through the coldest
bluest vein.
　　She, when the land labored
with flowers, their scent
flowing into her pores,
had molded her earth
like a woman
with soft breasted slopes
yielding silent mornings
and purple noisy birthings,
yellow hay
and tomatoes throbbing
like the sea.

And then
all was hushed for announcements:
    "Take only what you can carry ..."
We were made to believe
our faces betrayed us.
Our bodies were loud
with yellow
screaming flesh
needing to be silenced
behind barbed wire.

                    "Mr. Commissioner ...
                    ... it seems we were singled out
                    from others who were under suspicion.
                    Our neighbors were of German and Italian
                    descent, some of whom were not citizens ...
                    It seems we were singled out ..."

She had worn her sweat
like lemon leaves
shining on the rough edges of work,
removed the mirrors
from her rooms
so she would not be tempted
by vanity.
    Her dreams
honed the blade of her plow.
The land,
the building of food was
noisy as the opening of irises.
The sounds of work
bolted in barracks ...
silenced.

                    Mr. Commissioner ...
                    So when you tell me I must limit testimony
                    to 5 minutes, when you tell me my time is up,
                    I tell you this:
                    Pride has kept my lips
                    pinned by nails
                    my rage coffined.
                    But I exhume my past
                    to claim this time.
                    My youth is buried in Rohwer,
                    Obachan's ghost visits Amache Gate,
                    My niece haunts Tule Lake.
                    Words are better than tears,
                    so I spill them.
                    I kill this, the silence ...

190

There are miracles that happen,
she said,
and everything is made visible.
    We see the cracks and fissures in our soil:
We speak of suicides and intimacies,
of longings lush like wet furrows,
of oceans bearing us toward imagined riches,
of burning humiliations and
crimes by the government.
Of self hate and of love that breaks
through silences.
    We are lightning and justice.
    Our souls become transparent like glass
revealing tears for war-dead sons
red ashes of Hiroshima
jagged wounds from barbed wire.
    We must recognize ourselves at last
    We are a rainforest of color
and noise.
    We hear everything.
    We are unafraid.

                    Our language is beautiful.

(Quoted excerpts from my mother's testimony modified with her permission)

Breaking Tradition

for my Daughter

My daughter denies she is like me,
Her secretive eyes avoid mine.
    She reveals the hatreds of womanhood
      already veiled behind music and smoke and telephones.
I want to tell her about the empty room
    of myself.
    This room we lock ourselves in
    where whispers live like fungus,
    giggles about small breasts and cellulite,
    where we confine ourselves to jealousies,
    bedridden by menstruation.
    This waiting room where we feel our hands
    are useless, dead speechless clamps
    that need hospitals and forceps and kitchens
    and plugs and ironing boards to make them useful.
I deny I am like my mother. I remember why:
    She kept her room neat with silence,
    defiance smothered in requirements to be otonashii,
    passion and loudness wrapped in an obi,
    her steps confined to ceremony,
    the weight of her sacrifice she carried like
    a foetus. Guilt passed on in our bones.
I want to break tradition—unlock this room
    where women dress in the dark.
    Discover the lies my mother told me.
    The lies that we are small and powerless
    that our possibilities must be compressed
    to the size of pearls, displayed only as
    passive chokers, charms around our neck.
Break Tradition.
    I want to tell my daughter of this room
    of myself
    filled with tears of violins,
    the light in my hands,
    poems about madness,
    the music of yellow guitars—
    sounds shaken from barbed wire and
    goodbyes and miracles of survival.
    This room of open window where daring ones escape.
My daughter denies she is like me
    her secretive eyes are walls of smoke
    and music and telephones,
    her pouting ruby lips, her skirts
    swaying to salsa, teena marie and the stones,
    her thighs displayed in carnavals of color.
    I do not know the contents of her room.
She mirrors my aging.
She is breaking tradition.

Photo by Pierr Morgan

Jim Mitsui

Biographical/Poetics statement: "Poetry found me when I was 28, Presently I am finding out what it means to be a Northamerican. My favorite poet is James Wright. I very much admire Carolyn Forche's work, and what she is doing. Favorite recent book: ISLA NEGRA by Pablo Neruda."

Book publications:
JOURNAL OF THE SUN, Copper Canyon Press, 1974
CROSSING THE PHANTOM RIVER, Graywolf Press, 1978
AFTER THE LONG TRAIN, The Bieler Press, 1983

Shakuhachi

—for Ina San

When his son-in-law
asked for lessons,
he nodded.
Slipped the bamboo
out of its silk case.
Played one note.
Played it till it hung
clear as the moon.
Handed over the instrument.
Said, "Practice this note.
Come back in a year
for the second."

When Father Came Home for Lunch

I listen to my parent's language,
watch my father eat his separate meal,
the railroad motor car
cooling off and waiting
on the siding by the section house.
He sits with his back to the burning
woodstove in a captain's chair
and eats the family left-overs,
a bowl of rice balanced in his hand,
chopsticks flicking
around to the bowls & dishes
arranged in front of him.

Mother adds fried onions, a fried egg
and potatoes to his main bowl.
He adds catsup, shoyu
and mixes it with the white radish,
egg plant and cold chicken.
He works around to the mustard caked bowl
before each mouth of rice,
sauce hanging from his mustache.
Hot coffee, heavy with sugar & cream,
steams from a china mug.
Half-an-hour of noisy manners
and he's gone, back to work
in oily bib overalls.
I can still smell sweat
soaking his long-sleeved workshirt.

194

Letter to Tina Koyama from Elliot Bay Park

Last night at Bon Odori the drums of Kinnara Taiko
gathered in rhythm, and like startled birds
my thoughts spiraled away
from that street filled with kimonos & yukatas.
It's our poems, Tina. Some people are bothered
that literature seldom wins fame & money.
They worry that we're wasting our lives.
If they stood at the edge of discovering themselves,
at the rim of a great silence,
they would expect band music or blueprints.
Some kind of prize.
It is Monday afternoon.
Women dressed for offices
have brought sack lunches,
have taken off their shoes and found a place
in the grass. Behind my bench
a train thunders a deep song,
its engine creasing the stillness
with a horn that rhymes with commerce
& the echoing response of the outgoing
Winslow ferry. The bay is covered
with soft furrows. Off Bainbridge Island
tugboats pull a World War II battleship
toward a future as a missile carrier.
It will help protect the glass bank buildings
that climb over the backs of the old skyline.
Some men love the taste of money.
They would not care that my poems
help me become more Japanese, that they bring me
closer to memories that I thought had died
with my father. They would not believe
that poems have reasons that logic cannot comprehend.
Picking up my rucksack to leave,
I feel the sun rushing across the sky.
I feel the wind urging us on,
asking why we should expect to translate
the hunger of poetry.

Mexico City, 150 Pesos to the Dollar

1.

After the poetry of outwaiting the line-up
of immigration clerks
slouching in polyester, sliding under thoughts
of bribery, we land in the middle
of a freeway. It is a dirty, busy Oz.
Five minutes and the reputations & rusty fenders
of B.C. drivers
disappear in the oily smoke of buses
and a carnival of horns & speed.
Turn-signals might as well be Christmas lights.
Faded signs sigh "NO REBASE" at cars
fishtailing & ricocheting into the cloudy
catfish murk of night
under pink fluorescence.

2.

Insurgentes. Paseo de la Reforma.
At every stoplight you can buy Chiclets, vinyl
floor mats, sparklers, even chrome
B-29 bombers. There are no Salvation Armies here
only the redundancy of photo & optical shops.
It seems every beggar has a baby—I am told
some are hired for the day. Vendors
buff dusty shoes; serious Indian women
sell pumpkin seeds, Coke & black velvet art
a block away from the Zona Rosa
with its Gucchi, onyx and Toulouse-Lautrec.
This is the geography map I flew over
on Flight 740. I feel a quiz show embarrassment
at dollars that buy too much.
The world is becoming a lottery.

3.

Palm trees. Henry Moore & Picasso
at the museums. Even a French castle.
I study Diego Rivera's murals and forget
the absence of birds. On back streets
boys display magazines, shuffling hundreds of neon titles
down the sidewalk. The old smells of stone-ground meal
& chilis step out of courtyards.
My emotions are black & white
in a VW splash of color and the breathy wind
of panpipes. Cortes' remains age inside an obscure
church wall; the sign outside is retreating
behind an unpruned tamarind tree.

4.
It feels right—I don't believe in sharp knives
and the origins of the pyramids
at Teotihuacan are blurred.
We have driven here after having just admired
art deco buildings in the city.
The Pyramids of the Sun & Moon are stylized
echoes of the hills around this valley.
Walking up the Avenue of the Dead in a volcano-hush,
I look up. The sky hangs differently here.
A shadow empties the bottom of the moon.

16 February 1983

Graffiti in a University Restroom: "Killing People Is Easier than Writing Poetry"

"The river doesn't know it's called a river."
                    —Pablo Neruda

At school, during class,
I step out into the hall and hear film-track narratives
of preludes to war
flow out of social studies doors.
Last night,
sleeping alone,
I woke at 2 a.m.
and thought about our president,
made in Hollywood,
addressing an audience of evangelists,
asking them
to convince their congregations
that a nuclear freeze
is to lay down our weapons.
But we lay our weapons down
next to an arsenal of 8 world destructions,
people sleep under viaducts
and our leadership insulates itself
with advisors
who would look better in comic strips
than front pages
and hopefully not in newsreels
that will echo into the hallways of our future.
I wish politicians didn't know
they were called politicians.
I wish we wouldn't popularize products
made in Japan & Detroit
& Hollywood. I wish rivers
would talk to the world in a language
that even the creators of soundtracks
could understand.

Photo by Geoffrey Peckham

David Mura

David Mura received his B.A. from Grinnell College and did graduate work in English at the University of Minnesota. He won an American Academy of Poets award at the University of Minnesota State Arts Board grant (1980) and a Bush Foundation Fellowship (1981). His work has been published in the anothology, Brother Songs, *and in* The American Poetry Review, The Mississippi Review, The Chowder Review, Another Chicago Magazine, The Lake Street Review, *and* Sing, Heavenly Muse! *He has taught at the University of Minnesota and in the COMPAS Writers-in-the-Schools program. A sansei, both his parents were interred in the "relocation" camps during World War II.*

POETICS STATEMENT
"During the past year I have been moving away from a traditional blank verse line to poems that are more free form, sometimes even in prose. I seem in general to receive more sustenance from prose writers (Faulkner, Marquez, Kundera, Woolf, Barthes) than poets, perhaps because their influences are not so telling and because I want poetry to explore more possibilities than it currently does in America. In the past few years feminist writers have probably been more active than males in incorporating and formulating new insights in their poetry. Books like Susan Griffin's Pornography And Silence *just haven't seemed to penetrate the psyche of many male poets and I feel this is wrong. I'd like to see a male poetry emerge in this country which has the political and historical awareness of Milosz, the generosity and fallibility of Hikmet, and the communal, androgynous feeling of Whitman. The material and tools are there; it's time now to start building."*

199

The Hibakusha's Letter (1955)

Survivors of the atomic bomb were called hibakushas.
This name soon became associated with keloids, a whitish-
yellow scar tissue, and later, with defects, disease,
and disgrace.

The fields, Teruko-san, are threshed. A good
Harvest. All week I've seen farmers with torches
Bending to earth, releasing fires. The winds
Sweep ash across the roads, dirty my laundry
Hung on the fence. Prayer drums fill the streets,
And now the village starts to celebrate.
Last night Matsuo told me how he emptied
On a clump of rags beside the inn. Suddenly
The clump leaped up, groggy and cursing.
Matsuo finished, bowed, offered him a drink.
This morning I went out back to gossip
With my neighbor, an eighty-year old woman
Who prances like a mouse about her garden.
While she jabbered Matsuo cut her firewood;
Sweat poured from the scars he no longer marks.
Later I opened my shrine to its brass Buddha,
And fruit flies scattered from the bowl of plums
I've forgotten to change. Saved from the rubble,
Burnt at the edges, my fiance's picture
Crumbled in my fingers. I lit him incense.
Matsuo says we can't drag each corpse behind us
Like a shadow. The eye blinks, a world's gone,
And the slow shudder at our shoulders says
We won't be back. This year I've changed my diet
And eat only rice, utskemono, tofu.
Sashimi sickens me, passion for raw meat.
Sister, remember how mother strangled chickens?
She twirled them in the air by their necks
Like a boy with a sling-shot. I'd watch in horror
Their bodies twitch, hung from her fist, and cry
That Buddha laid their karma in my stomach.
Like them we had no warning. Flames filled kimonos
With limbs of ash, and I wandered beneath
Smouldering torriis away from the city.
Of course you're right. We can't even play beauty
Or the taste of steel quickens our mouths.
I can't conceive, and though Matsuo says
It doesn't matter, my empty belly haunts me:
Why call myself a woman, him a man,
If on our island only ghosts can gather?
And yet, I can't deny it. There are times,
Teruko, I am happy ...
You say hibakushas should band together. Here

Fewer eyes cover us in shame. I wandered
Too far: My death flashed without, not within.
I can't come back. To beg the world's forgiveness
Gains so little, and monuments mean nothing.
I can't choose your way or even Matsuo's:
"Drink, Michiko, sake's the one surgeon
Doesn't cost or cut." Today, past fields black
And steaming, the pitch of night soil, I'll walk
Almost at peace. After a wind from hell,
The smell of burning now seems sweeter than flowers.

Lan Nguyen: The Uniform of Death
1971

At the jungle's edge, torn open
near the neck, the carcass of a dog.
Five hissing flies bathe in the wound.
Brush them away and tiny white worms
swim like grains of rice in a soup
of blood. Still fresh enough to eat.
I hack off the head.

At night, in a row down the road, a hundred heads.
Dust swirls around them, little whirlwinds,
and I hear the heads breathing,
humming, indecipherable murmurs, a foreign tongue.
They stop: a high scream like a woman's—

My hand's at my mouth
to clamp it shut.

In the river, my face
is twisted, mottled green,
a mango rotted eight days in the jungle's oven.
I splash the water, wait to clear.

Only water, only water.

Where is the man's face I dragged to the fire?
Through his screams, I saw skin bubble and blacken.
Ground the head down farther, felt flames
hiss at my wrists, let go—
It fell with a thump, sparks jumped, I
held them in my palms.

Licking my fingertips,
I smelled his face.

Cutting sliver after sliver
from the branches of the balsam,
we fashioned a cage for crickets.
They sang each night
beside a jar of fireflies.
When my brother knocked them from the table,
they spread out like sparks of a flare
before the copters darted down river,
wings beating ...

Flares, fireflies, flares, fireflies ...

If you cut its legs, a cricket,
since it sings from its legs,
just rocks, silent on its belly;
but tear each limb from his sockets,
a man still sings out with a burst of his lungs.

I think we should fight underwater,
crawling at the river bottom,
moving heavily, flies caught in honey.
Always, no matter how much blood
oozes out in murky clouds, no matter how
the faces freeze in the last gulp
for air, no matter how much you want
to mourn, your brother in your hands,
nothing cries out—only the thick thunder
of the current moves in your ears.

Not with a light tap on the shoulder
but with a tiny cylinder of lead
hurled so fast it knocks a man flat,
I mark men unfit for life;
so many, I ask the figure
who will call me from life—
Who is the imposter?
Who wears the uniform of death?

Relocation

for Grandfather Uyemura

People married by pictures then;
when they lied, the bride stepped
from the ship and found a dwarf,
nose gnarled as a ginger root.

He was so handsome, he came
in person, held her as America rose
and fell ahead. Gulls shrieked;
on the dock, the pale ghosts gathered.

*

He bought a greenhouse on a field
hand's wages, and with Cuban cigar
jammed in his jaw, watched his
orchids like petulant courtesans.

Nights, the eucalyptus swayed,
his eyes gleamed with his Packard's
chrome beneath the moon. He slapped his
thighs, rubbed the dirt from his hands,

prayed for dice clicking sevens.
By dawn he was whistling home.
He stumbled in roses,
said hello to the thorns.

*

When they shipped him like cattle
to the camps, he sat in the mess hall
and creased a napkin like the nine-ply
folds of heaven; out of his hands

flew a slim, white crane. His wife
shook her head, smiled, forgot barbed
wire, guards. At a mule-pulled plow
he wiped his baseball cap across

his brow, looked past the wires to
the prairie where the west begins. Tipping
his cap to the corporal in the tower,
he muttered "Baka," picked up the reins.

He named his son Kitsugi, prince
of birds. After the war it was Tom,
such a strange name, like someone
beating a drum, hollow, a hard echo.

He laughed at the boy's starving
Jesus, nails piercing the little bones
of the hands and feet, told him
the Buddha always ate well.

When she died, he returned to Tokyo.
Still attached to his body, limbs
folded on a chair, he spent
his evenings composing haiku—

> *Bansai tree,*
> *like me you are useless*
> *and a little sad.*

The Natives

Several months after we lost our way,
they began to appear, their quiet eyes
assuring us, their small painted legs
scurrying beside us. By then our radio
had been gutted by fungus, our captain's cheek
stunned by a single bullet; our ammo vanished
the first night we discovered our maps were useless,
our compasses a lie. (The sun and stars
seemed to wheel above us, each direction
north, each direction south.) The second week
forced us on snakes, monkeys, lizards, and toads;
we ate them raw over wet smoking fires.
Waking one morning we found a river boat
loaded with bodies hanging in the trees
like an ox on a sling, marking the stages
of flood. One of us thought he heard the whirr
of a chopper, but it was only the monsoon
drumming the leaves, soaking our skin so damp
you felt you could peel it back to scratch
the bones of your ankle. Gradually our names
fell from our mouths, never heard again.
Nights, faces glowing, we told stories of wolves,
and the jungle seemed colder, more a home.

And then we glimpsed them, like ghosts of children
darting through the trees, the curtain of rain;
we told each other nothing, hoping they'd vanish.
But one evening the leaves parted. Slowly
they emerged and took our hands, their striped
faces dripping, looking up in wonder
at our grizzled cheeks. Stumbling like gods
without powers, we carried on our backs
what they could not carry, the rusted grenades,
the ammoless rifles, barrels clotted with flies.
They waited years before they brought us
to their village, led us in circles till
time disappeared. Now, stone still, our feet
tangled with vines, we stand by their doorways
like soft-eyed virgins in the drilling rain:
the hair on our shoulders dangles and shines.

A Nisei Picnic

In these ambiguous photos, their faces gaze
forever at the sun. A picnic basket
opens before them; ants crawl in the slats.

Here is my uncle, a rice ball in his mouth.
Eventually he ballooned like Buddha,
over three hundred pounds. I used to stroke
his immense belly, which was scarred by shrapnel.
It made me feel patriotic.
For two nights he lay in a ditch near the Danube
and held in his intestines with his hands.
When he came back, he couldn't rent an apartment.
"*Shi-ka-ta-ga-nai,*" he said. *It can't be helped.*

Turning from her boyfriend, a glint of giggle
caught in the shadows, my aunt never married.
On the day of her wedding, sitting in the bath,
she felt her knees lock; she couldn't get up.
For years I wanted to be her son.
She took me to zoos, movies, bought me candy.
When I grew up she started raising minks
in her basement—"To make money," she said—
Most of them died of chills. She folded each one
in a shoebox and buried it in her yard.

My father's the one pumping his bicep.
(Sleek, untarnished, he still swims two miles a day.)
I can't claim that his gambling like his father
lost a garage, greenhouse or grocery,
or that, stumbling drunk, he tumbled in
the bushes with Mrs. Hoshizaki, staining
his tuxedo with mulberries and mud. He
worked too hard to be white. He beat his son.

Shown here, my head like a moon dwarfing my body
as I struggle to rise. Who are these grownups?
Why are they laughing? How can I tear
the bewilderment from their eyes?

Photo by Clyde Okita

Dwight Okita

I was born on August 26, 1958. It is now 1982 and I am still here. I write the kind of poems that I like to read: visual, approachable. The sort of thing that might be fun finding in an old whiskey bottle along the shore, if you were stranded on an island.

The Art of Holding On

So this is Monday.
I open my door and there it is
with the mail: ready, waiting.
And if I step into it like a taxi
will it take me somewhere,
can I roll down the windows
and shout my name as loud as it will go?
I open my hand and feel for rain.
I climb in.
Here we go, hold on.

Marcie slips into Wednesday
like a new dress. It flatters her
and she looks on the bright side,
looks at a map and wonders where
her priorities lie.
All these roads, she says.
By evening she is there
and she can count on one finger
all the reasons she came.

Frank likes his Fridays,
wants to hold them in his hands
like pencils and see if they write.
Tonight he will call me out of the blue
and tell me he has made plans for the evening
and I am part of them. See you at 6:00.
The day spins on its edge
and drops like a penny
to the sidewalk—call it.
Heads.

Crossing with the Light

All these nights, all these traffic lights.
And love, that busy street.

And scientists would stand in white coats and talk
amongst themselves about the Doppler Effect:
how love takes longer to arrive than to depart,
a car approaching in the oncoming lane, what happens
when source and observer are drawing closer together.

And poets would see love in the parking of a car,
love in the rear-view mirror, love in the slowing
of tires between yellow lines.
"Stay with me in this parking lot," the driver
would say. "All my life, I have held this space
for someone like you."

Meanwhile back at the curb,
we were waiting.

I wanted to stand here and watch
the city run out of things to say
and the cars out of gas
till everything was stopped—
and you would be the first thing to move.

But nights like these, you can look both ways
and still not see it coming. Nights like these
you want to walk away from headlights,
kiss the concrete goodnight as a gentleman would.

Meanwhile back at the curb . . .
we were crossng. Slowly at first but crossing
shoes lifting over pavement, steady as rain
"Red Rover, Red Rover, let . ."
That someone would be waiting on the other side—
not waiting to cross, not waiting for signs
waiting only for you this time.

Something in your stride asks,
"This one? This time? Is *this* it?"
And a voice that comes from the street,
from the cracks in the sidewalk,
from the curb you stand on and all the curbs
you've ever stood on and waited at—
a voice that says,
"Yes. This one. This time. This is the place."

In Response to Executive Order 9066:
ALL AMERICANS OF JAPANESE DESCENT MUST REPORT TO RELOCATION CENTERS

Dear Sirs:
Of course I'll come. I've packed my galoshes
and three packets of tomato seeds. Janet calls them
"love apples." My father says where we're going
they won't grow.

I am a fourteen-year-old girl with bad spelling
and a messy room. If it helps any, I will tell you
I have always felt funny using chopsticks
and my favorite food is pizza.
My best friend is a white girl named Denise—
we look at boys together. She sat in front of me
all through grade school because of our names:
O'Connor, Ozawa. I know the back of Denise's head very well.
I tell her she's going bald. She tells me I copy on tests.
We are best friends.

I saw Denise today in Geography class.
She was sitting on the other side of the room.
"You're trying to start a war," she said, "giving secrets away
to the Enemy, Why can't you keep your big mouth shut?"
I didn't know what to say.
I gave her a packet of tomato seeds
and asked her to plant them for me, told her
when the first tomato ripens
to miss me.

Parachute

"...nights opening
out farther and farther, like the billowing
of a parachute, with only that slit
Of starlight."
—John Ashbery
"Litany"

I

At night, the coffeepot stands upended in the rack.
A nightlight turns its seashell back to the room
and spreads its light on a wall.
Rubberbands hang quiet around a doorknob.
These are the Certain Hours and for a while I know
where I stand in a house, I'm sure of it.
But then the coffeepot rights itself
and begins singing the old song. My feet lower
to the inevitable wood floor, to the new day.
All year, I have practiced this jump.

II

Frank and I sit on the swings in an empty schoolyard
tonight. We face opposite ways and he watches me
as we meet at the bottom of our arcs, watches me
get smaller and farther away. I slow, let the rubber seat
slide up under the back of my knees, hang there
looking at my shoes, stars. "So what's your story?" he says
hanging low in his seat now as I do.
"I have no story," I say and look at the blacktop moving
beneath me, watch Frank getting smaller
and farther away.
I have no story. I have these chains and I hold them.

III

They say these evenings open up like parachutes
and each night someone is saved:
by string, white cloth filling with air
snagging on the sky.
But I say these nights fall like card houses
in the wind, the cards swirl at your feet.
A nightlight turns its seashell back to the room.

Photo by A. Framer

Mark Osaki

Biographical statement
   I was born in 1952.

Poetics statement
   I believe that attention to craft must supersede careless construction (poor thinking), "special effects," and intellectual dishonesty, i.e., themes fashioned to correspond to trendy moral or popular precepts which are at once cynical and self-congratulatory.
   The major theme of my poetry is that of moral ambiguity: the realization that ethical considerations—even when we don't recognize them as such—compel us toward a confrontation of some kind. That even when one attempts a moral course, one can discover that, as with a Mobius strip, good intentions often lead logically to corruption. All my poems deal with these discoveries or confrontations.
   Good structure, subtlety, and clear thinking insure good writing. If I am in any way successful in achieving this in my poetry, it is largely due to Leonard Nathan, whose sure and eloquent voice is certainly one of the finest in American poetry today.

List of publications
   My poetry has appeared in publications in the U.S. and abroad, including: The Georgia Review, Impulse Press, Contemporary Quarterly, S.H.Y. *(Greece),* South Carolina Review, Strath Poetry Journal *(Scotland),* Studies in Poetry, Three Rivers Poetry Journal, Wisconsin Review, *and* Zvezda.
   I have received awards for my poetry from the University of California, Berkeley, and the Academy of American Poets. I received a Creative Writing Fellowship Grant from the National Endowment for the Arts in 1982. I was nominated for a 1983-84 Guggenheim Fellowship earlier this year.
   I recently completed a book of poems entitled Tradecraft.

For Avi Killed in Lebanon

Long distance is expensive
so the messages were short.
First the call from the consulate,
then confirmation by telegram:
the best Jew in the service
has auctioned off the kibbutz.

Few here let out war whoops.
It was bound to happen had
you stayed with us and not defected.
You were finally overtaken by the
same choice we all made years ago,
when a dutiful and pretentious bastard
could see the road going on forever.

In Cairo, you pointed to a wash of stars
and marvelled at how people could be
duped into believing in them long after
they had grown cold and dead, light
taking so long to reach us.
Our business was like that—to keep
the morons guessing, you said.

Death has lost its random aspects,
and there is nothing more unprofessional
than faith. Still Avrum, my beloved
old friend, sometimes pretense is the light
which fills the enormity of the sky.

Icon

Once, in a great while,
you will see a sign
and invest in it everything
out of simple faith
it is meant for you.

You will surrender
all you've been taught
to the purity of its direction
and stand perfectly still
knowing nothing more is beyond it.

This is how they will find you:
unable to break away, peering
steadfast from the threshold,
starved by certainty,
blessed forever and unobserved.

Amnesiac

For awhile I too was haunted by
memories of your frightened faces
as we hovered nearby, shooting
warning tracers above your heads.
It was amazing—you thought waving
American flags would save you.

We had other rooftops to fly to.
Coming back from the last one we
saw the fire you had set as a beacon.
We couldn't help it. We laughed.

The cries and curses you threw up
into that sky were instantly
drowned out and chopped up
by bladed arks already flying away.

I am among my own now, who do not
worship stones or rivers, or impute
to them a memory of any kind.
What does not perish here by forgetting
survives only in the occasional bad dream.

We wake up each morning to a new history.
We don't know if we remember.

Turista

From the veranda I watch the jetsam
of another election
flash before me like gunfire.
Perhaps out of guilt, I promise myself
a sticky slice of fried banana for every
body that is crumpled against the blackened
wall in the courtyard below.

Back home, a man my age is voting
for the first time. Here a sentry
is positioned on every rooftop
to remind the electorate who won.
I would wave, but they have seen enough
of my hands moving under the skirts
of this inherited country.

Already, I am thinking of Paris, my reward.
I take another warm section of fruit
and compose my next cable:
Situation improving. Stop. They're using
our rifles.

Contentment

None of our warnings sank in.
He was already celebrating
the reunion at the border, his
daughter's first ballet lessons,
the promise of the other side.

We've all dreamed of that crossing:
a river to erase our tracks, the
welcome in the clearing just ahead,
the guide who becomes our one love.
Years spent accustomed to others
failing has brought us quiet relief
in not making the effort.

Days later we followed his trial
in the papers and made cruel jokes
about the clothesline he had carried,
not half what he would have needed.
After the rains, the only sign that
remained was a girl's weathered shoe
still caught in the wire.

Elsewhere, perhaps it makes sense to
have a destination worth so much risk.
Possible even to make good an escape
with a rope so short it seems fit
only for a hanging.

Richard Oyama

Richard Oyama was born and raised in New York City. From 1974-1978, he was the coordinator of the Basement Writers Workshop, an Asian American community arts organization in Chinatown, NY. His work has appeared in Quilt, Y'Bird, downbeat, Bridge, Sunbury *and other publications. He also co-edited* American Born and Foreign, *an anthology of Asian American poetry, published by Sunbury Press. Oyama has a Master's degree in English: Creative Writing from San Francisco State University. In June 1983, he will be conducting a writing workshop through an NEA writer-in-residence grant at Basement Workshop. Oyama currently lives in San Francisco.*

The Day After Trinity

"I am become death, the shatterer of worlds"
—J. Robert Oppenheimer quoting a passage
from Hindu scripture after the Trinity bomb test

1.

August 6, 1945.   City of Hiroshima
(once a Buddhist castle town.

The cross-winged shadow of Enola Gay falls
across the city
an American "Fat Boy" drops
through the warm air.

A flash of blue light sears the empty sky
(that flash becomes an indelible scar
along the curved bone of our skulls

Tile-roofed wooden houses collapse
in a flaming sea
a false twilight descends
the city veiled in black rain.

Daylight consigned to
an eternity of night.
Black plague.   Blindness.   No escape.

The dead flood the banks
of the seven rivers.
Paper lanterns float
down the Ohta River.

"Mizu, mizu, mizu,"
chant the fleshless ghosts.

Only the shadow of a man imprinted
on the concrete steps of Sumitomo Bank.

2.

Two minutes after eleven o'clock
on the morning of August 9th
a second atomic bomb is
dropped on Nagasaki.

3.

At the base of the Children's Monument
for Sadako Sasaki flowing with
multicolored streamers like willows of
a thousand cranes   the inscription:

"This is our cry
this is our prayer
peace in the world."

This is the day after Trinity when
ten thousand suns explode.

(Note: mizu is the Japanese word for water).

Richard Oyama 219

Obon By The Hudson

Behind the New Jersey shore
the sun flames
windows of buildings flashing

gold high on the Palisade Cliffs
cars speed along the West Side
Highway homeward by

the waters of the Hudson
In this stone mall on Riverside Drive
the dancers fan themselves with bamboo

slatted paper fans and wipe their brows
on the shore of this river
From a worn phonograph

the long-ago sound of Japanese folk songs
Their arms in sharp-edged sleeves of kimonos
the dancers wheel in opposite directions

the graceful motion   gesture in unison
sumi-e on threads of rice paper
stepping in the twin moons of the dance

Dreams In Progress

I. The Secret Temple

Behind the Kokusai Theatre in Nihonmachi
there is a cobblestone stairway.
You will not find it.

I am walking up the winding stone steps
and enter the tree-shadowed grounds of
an ancient Buddhist temple.

There are shrines on the temple grounds.
In this distance
I see my father sit silent in meditation

having found the serenity he had not
known before.
I, too, am serene.

II. Peyote

Huge thunderhead clouds billow
above the Arizona desert
a meeting of tribes of all nations.
Heat shimmers in waves above the sand

spiky cacti patterned along
a landscape with no horizon
while the car radio sings
"I been through the desert on

a horse with no name . . ."
In Jerome, Jean, our Canadian driver, bought
a bushel of peyote
buttons he planned to sell in San Francisco.

"Peyote is a sacrament
to our people," the Indian tells him.
We had picked him up
hitching along Big Sur.

He had just gotten out of the joint.

III. Sundown, New Mexico

Far off from the road
flat mesas silhouetted black against
the sun's last light

a sky stained water colors
layered in luminous bands of
pinks, reds and oranges vibrating

the uppermost sky hard
and blue as turquoise

IV.   Into The Fog

Fog charges over Twin Peaks
ghost buffaloes across the plains
cool evening
                    deep into blues
electric lights from houses they are stars
scattered
              along the hills

Fog blowing wet
mist against my face   it is
unheard music
of the wind   it has
taken my mind away

This Song Shows Me Pictures:
Morningside Drive, New York City
1950–1960

1.

White curtains blowing inward.

2.

Grey shapes slip silent across
the ceiling.

3.

My bed faces the window:
a rectangle of yellow light shining
from streetlamps four
floors below.
I dream in technicolor.

4.

In this photograph
my father's face appears gaunt
his cheekbones prominent
like that of an Indian, one hand in
the pocket of his grey wool overcoat.
The three of us stand in front of him
around a see-the-view telescope.
Behind us, the stone wall,
the river, and the country landscape.
Carrie smiles shyly, cheeks dimpled,
peeking, leaning out behind Bob.
I'm dressed in a blue synthetic jumpsuit,
my face puzzled, my cupped hand extended
for something.
Confidently smiling, eye slitted to
aim, Bob is pointing his toy gun
into the camera lens.

5.

"I gave my love a cherry," she sings,
"that had no stone." My mother has the
sweetest voice I have ever heard. I love
this song, it shows me pictures.
Cherries have no stones.
I walk under a big overhanging stone cliff,
clouded ice flowing over rock surface
dripping water, across the street
from P.S. 125.

6.

"They took me to the railroad station
in the middle of the desert. Middle of
nowhere. They took me there and
left me. They told me
nothing. They didn't tell me
I was going to spend the week with
relatives," his voice telling me
this story in the dark. I have heard
it before. I see
the train station, a small black square
on the indistinct horizon between
desert and sky, yellow dust blowing
along the boundless landscape.
He goes from my bedside and I am
left to dream.

7.

The magician performs tricks in
Macy's toy department.
I know all of the tricks and
shout out how they're done.
The magician, dressed in a
striped red-and-white jacket
and face shadowed with beard, gives me
an evil look. I'm ruining
his act. Later, Mrs. Tanbara buys
me a new trick. When we get
home, I practice my magic.

8.

Mom and Dad are having a fight.
I run into Mrs. Tanbara's room.
There is a silk screen on the
left side of the door. I practice
magic tricks on her bed, call her
Granma, even though she's only an
old Issei woman who boards with us.
My father calls her "unobtrusive."
Tired, I become quarrelsome, throw
tantrums, kick her in the stomach.
Confused, she doesn't understand me.
Unable to do anything else, she throws me
in the closet, locks it. It's dark
inside, I bang my fists on the door
pleading with her to let me out.

9.

"Doctor Livingston, I presume?"
The movie on television is over.
Fever has taken hold.
I am deep in Africa somewhere.
Skin of my face is melting from bone.
Talk-drums are throbbing in my brain.
My blue pajamas are drenched in sweat.
I spit gouts of blood into a bucket.
I rise from my bed, staggering out
into the hall.
"Doctor Livingston, I presume?"
"Doctor Livingston, I presume?"
"Doctor Livingston, I presume?"
The river flooded with huge iridescent pearls
threatens to engulf me.

10.

I am looking out of the livingroom window.
Outside, a gold ocean glimmering in sun.
I have this dream over and over.
When I wake up, the ocean is gone. The scene
outside the window remains the same. Blacktops
of rows upon rows of Harlem tenements
clotheslines sagging, wet sheets blowing
in cold wind, smoke curling from
a smokestack into grey winter sky, red
and green neon of a huge billboard blinking
on, off. No ocean. Mom and Dad grew up in
California. I have never been there.

Al Robles

born in s.f. ifugao mountain wood and rock collector. now involved in collecting carabao tales with ragged patches of the first pilipinos, old-timers—manongs, in america—in a place called manilatown where the smell of chicken blood fills the air—where adobo soaks up your tribal vision—where pig entrails dangle like rosary beads from the sky—where dreams of the tribal past echo—where carabaos dance on each rice grain— where the taste of life is in the heart of fish tales and loincloth rituals— where brown hands meet the moon together.

published in yarbird, yardbird pub., 1975., time to greeze, third world publication, 1974., liwanag, liwanag press, 1976. art and literature, vol. 1 & vol. 2., japan publication, 1970. looking for ifugao mountain, children's press, 1976., Other—sources: an american essay, art institute pub., 1975., ode to bill sorro, pub. in osaka, japan, 1974., asian american authors, mifflin/houghton pub. 1973., texas long grain, kearny st. press, 1983., contemporary poets of america, piece and pieces pub. 1975. counter-point: asian-american literature, 1973., asian roots, 1976. forthcoming book: kayaomunggi vision of a wandering carabao, 1983—isthmus foundation publication.

Sushi-Okashi and Green Tea with Mitsu Yashima

cherry blossom spring festival
outside yashima's window
a cedar sways
looking northeast
remnants of konnyaku's past
a buried tea house
under a slab of cement
splintered bamboo memories
rise up in the fog
nihonmachi tambourines
turn into kokeshi dolls
hidden behind moth-eaten shinto robes
michiko's koto strings break the silence
taiko drums
pound mochi
into snow
mitsu yashima
born in kobe
california-1950
seventy-five years old issei woman—
oh ageless child!
swim the river
in the sky
  "i want to be free from everything—
                    from everybody."

i hear
your brush stokes
in the wind
painting a river
in the sky
drinking the tea
sushi and manju
we need not ask for more
only our tea cups
remained empty
yashima-san
your laughter moves
a thousand hokkaido mountains
i'll carry a thousand pound sushi
for you—and scatter manju to flying cranes,
in the spring rain.

Manong Federico Delos Reyes
and His Golden Banjo

back home
in the p.i.
i ride the snake
i ride the monkey
i ride the waterbuffalo
i ride the lizard
i ride the fish
i ride the coconut tree
in america
i ride the southern pacific box car
montana snow-bound cries
shuffling brown feet
in centerville taxi dance halls
i chase after the white women
in manilatown
i ride the stool
at blanco's bar
scotch on the rocks express
dreaming of dark brown pinays
i ride the seven seas
1920-golden banjo
strumming
songs of romance

"yes sir—that's my baby
   no sir—i don't mean maybe
yes sir—that's my baby doll."

silver wing cafe
"oh mama!
you got my fishhead?
and two plates of rice ..."

> oh god, how i love my fishhead!
> oh god, how i love my women!
> oh god, how i love my music!

Manong Jacinto Santo Tomas

when the first sound of the
carabao is heard—all is clear
like pearls in the bottom of
the bajou sea.

o'y o'y. come help me. hold dat one.
hand and dry dat fish in my room. first
i soak it in vinegar and salt. i cut from
da head down. spread like bird wings. if you
got plenty of dat one you lay dem flat inside
bathtub. da others you hang with dat rope."

    "why i no can do dat?
    Who tell me like dat?
    those people who eat with dat fork."

smile
manong jacinto
you gave
your
black thumb
to the rice gods
(who cares looking at the stars now, when you
                    can swallow each one).

manong
pound
the kulingtangs
rise up
in
your
cagayan loincloth
eat with carabao-winter hands.

    "Why i got these for — my hands?
    who give them to me?
    the rice and fish taste better dat way."

Boyang the Wandering Recluse

Boyang-Boyang-Boyang-Boyang-Boyang
The northern wind sweeps the mind clear
into a thousand dreams, drawing Boyang
farther & farther & deeper & deeper in-
to the "snows of life"—your bamboo
flute cuts across, echoes, and cuts
thru the thick icebergs—vibrating lay-
ers of the mind that circles the Baring Sea.
Loneliness grabs the heart, filling it with
burning portraits of "women of the past."
How many women have given their lives up
for you? ... their minds sweetened your taste
buds—their pale bodies clung to your wander-
ing bamboo flute.

Boyang-Boyang-Boyang-Boyang-Boyang
How deep is the silence of winter?
How far is the journey?
When the paths covered in snow
No longer welcome the ancient songs
Your long bamboo flute brings back snow-memories
Has the snow fallen?
Mountains grow tall and sad
Flowers waiting to bloom
Frozen silence
Still-dreams
Boyang-Boyang-Boyang-Boyang-Boyang
The snow is still thick around
Your bamboo flute.

A Mountain-Toilet Thief

A mountain-toilet thief
    ran off with Mee Har's breasts
Mee Har carries a mountain
    of sadness
           in each breast
and it sagged
and the birds wailed, wailed, wailed
               loud

Winter-Buddha face
         yellow autumn-skin
Empty mountain-breasts
        lips wet as early spring
and tight as two ripe persimmons
I am a wild mountain-toilet thief —
    ran off with Mee Har's
        young mountain-breasts

Four seasons   turned the soil
Scattered a thousand saplings
Fog covered the past
Left a young mountain-breast
        with the emptiness
of Buddha
Wiped Buddha clean with toilet paper
      and threw it to the wind.

Cathy Song

I was born in Honolulu, Hawaii in 1955. I hold degrees from Wellesley College and Boston University. My first book, Picture Bride *(Yale University Press) won the Yale Series of Younger Poets Award in 1982. After living in Cambridge, Massachusetts for the past seven years, I have returned home to Hawaii where I live with my husband, Dr. Douglas Davenport, and our one-year old son, Joshua.*

Lucky

The baby brought us luck
from the day we brought him home.
White curtains lifted
to let in the pale lemon light.

We hung his hat on the doorknob
and raised a flag
in the shape of a fish.

The man selling corn,
the woman folding sheets,
smiled and waved their approval.
The nurse left a poem in the mailbox.

Those who visited tiptoed around
the light that had landed in our living room.
The drunk declined his usual drink.
The lady with the many bracelets
stopped her jangling in mid-gesture.
It was as if they were entering a church.

We succumbed to sleep,
the three of us and slept
through the long mornings cool
with magnolias opening beneath our window.

His small hand curled around my thumb.
When I opened his rosebud fist, I found,
already etched, a complex map of his future.

My breasts were sweet for days.
The smell of milk
enticed a trail of black ants
to migrate out of the Boston fern.
Like a moving signature
weaving across the carpet,
it was his first alphabet.

Who Makes the Journey

In most cases,
it is the old woman
who makes the journey;
the old man having had
the sense to stay
put and die at home.

You see her scurrying
behind her
newly arrived family.
She comes from the Azores
and she comes from the Orient.
It makes no difference.
You have seen her before:

the short substantial
legs buckle
under the weight
of the ghost child
she carried centuries

ago like a bundle of rags
who now turns in front
of your windshield,
transformed in Western clothes.

The grown woman stops
impatiently
and self-consciously
to motion *Hurry* to her mother.

Seeping into your side view
mirror like a black mushroom
blooming in a bowl of water,
the stooped gnome figure
wades through the river
of cars hauling

her sack of cabbages,
the white and curved,
translucent leaves of which
she will wash individually
as if they were porcelain cups.

Like black seed buttons
sewn onto a shapeless dress,
those cryptic eyes
rest on your small reflection

for an instant. Years pass.
History moves like an old woman
crossing the street.

The Day You are Born

There was an emptiness
    waiting for you. The night
        your mother knew you existed,
she felt a flicker of sadness
    for the life, no bigger than her thumbnail,
        burrowing itself within her body.
She knew you would be
    her last child, the last flowering
        before the pod like a crippled hand,
withered shut; the body becoming silent.
    The eggs mature and ripe,
        pungent and salty as caviar.

The night she knew
    of your existence, the small town
        slept in the blue black darkness
of the eucalyptus trees and orchids.
    There was no moon to light
        the road your father would take,
spiraling in slow circles toward home.
    The key to his tailor shop
        hung from his neck like a cross.
He wore it constantly
    and the expression that went with it:
        the mournful mask of an immigrant.

If, upon returning,
    he went to the room where she slept,
        instead of walking past her door
carrying his shoes like a thief,
    he might have witnessed
        something of the grief she felt
for you who would be
    his third son, his fifth child.
        The boy who would dream
of airplanes as he crossed the river at night,
    his left hand assured
        by the worn railing of the bridge.
He would come to know its varied surface
    as it led him to the field
        where the bombers maneuvered
in the searchlit sky.
    There in that field
        you dreamed of the names
of the places you had picked
    like matches and marbles
        from the wireless
as the planes disappeared,
    leaving the sound of their engines
        and a boy turning slowly homeward.

They were to call you
    their thin soldier of the homefront
        where you were to remain
interpreting the war news for your father
    who would be by then already old.
        You would always think of him as old,
sitting in his chair,
    swatting the flies with a newspaper
        while you pinpointed on the map
the complicated names of islands
    with letters as numerous
        as the legs of an insect.
Islands where your two brothers crept
    on their bellies in a blue black darkness
        that reminded them of home.

Each morning you would come
    to stand before the injustice of love
        as your mother dressed her thin soldier
in an immaculate white starched shirt.
    Each night she steam pressed
        the collar with a hiss.
The sound of the iron seemed
    to sear a hole in your heart.
        And the punishment it brought
when like a sickly angel
    you descended upon the chicken
        dirt of the schoolyard.
Impressed by the mother who dressed
    her child like an angel,
        the teacher kept you at your desk
during the noon recess. The maps
    you drew flowered freely in your hand.
        She sent you home as a spotless example
although you delayed your departure
    until the huddle of children scattered,
        comfortable in their anonymous rags.

Your father would die uneventfully,
    but your mother, perched on the porch
        with a piece of sewing on her lap,
would be there waiting
    for a boy to walk home
        in the late afternoon light,
dragging his leather satchel
    behind him as if it was an anchor
        from which his shadow would rise
magnified and serene.
    The wind blows with the sound of eggshells
        the day you are born.

Losing Track

Last night, I saw a documentary
on China. The camera crew
had traveled to the far western
province of Xinjiang. In the brief
green meadows of summer in the hills,
I thought I recognized you,
for a moment, but it was a young girl
who could have been your sister.
She was leaping in a game,
trying to catch the tail's end, a small boy,
in a snake of children
weaving through the tall grass.
Her long braids were flying like the tassels
tying her cotton quilted vest.
The camera almost touched her face:
sturdy and earnest,
she seemed to smile against her will.

But of course it wasn't you.
If you have remained in China,
you would be pedaling an antique
bicycle in Beijing. I received two letters.
The students were so polite
they made you feel venerable
beyond your years, waiting after class
to hand you rice cakes and panfried doughnuts.
I can hear them reciting
your stilted English sentences: at school,
I had once mistaken you for a foreigner,
your speech was halting and deliberate.
You described your room, writing
how cold it was to face
the northern slant of the sun.
Sometimes, the light made you
think of Michigan,
driving home through the woods with your father.
You made tentative plans to return
to the family house,
to finish a book of stories
you began writing in an upstairs room.
And then you wrote
that you had fallen in love
with one of your students, but,
as if thinking it over,
you were riding an inland train
with someone else, a safe companion;
a woman with unfeminine features.

That is where we lost track
of one another. The silence that followed
your last letter grew longer,
becoming a tunnel of snow
the train you were riding whistled through.
Our words had been what had kept
us alive to one another and when they stopped,
a jade fish, an old coin,
was dropped into the blue China Sea.
Last night, I found myself alone,
watching television and not thinking
of anything in particular when
your face was brought back to life.
I dreamt I went to find you again
in the drafty hallways of the school
where in the mausoleum silence
of the library we would study, side by side,
like bookends; our identical hair
covering the English language we both loved.

The story you began writing in Michigan
was a notebook you carried
across the snow quiet fields of the campus.
Walking in the shadow of the lights
along College Road, our tracks
had already begun to diverge
with our good night and a stack of books
at the frozen lily pond.
I watched you trudge up the hill
toward the observatory.
I see you as you were then,
so serious you did not mean to scowl;
your black ponytail, an ink brush,
dipping into the night air,
dotting the points to a constellation
you had yet to name.

Luis Syquia

I was born in San Francisco in 1949—An original SF 49'er. Went to college at San Francisco State University and by meeting other Asian-Americans and taking a number of ethnic studies classes there, I became aware of the histories as well as the rich cultural heritage people of color have contributed to this country. Have worked at various jobs including; reporter/broadcast journalist for KPFA Berkeley (1976-77); spent two seasons working in Alaska, the last time as a butcher of King Crab in the Aleutian Islands during the Winter of '76. Most recently I worked at City Lights bookstore for 3½ years.

Have worked in various community projects including the International Hotel in SF and Agbayani Retirement Village in Delano. Edited a newsletter for a grass-roots Pilipino agency dealing w/ the problems of youth, recent immigrants and Senior citizens. Lectured on Pilipino-American Literature and gave poetry readings at University of the Philippines, Oakland Museum, U.C. Berkeley, UCLA, Sacto State, University of Santa Cruz and other colleges and cultural events up & down the West Coast for the past ten years or more.

My major source for ideas and inspiration comes from working and living, as well as interacting on a regular basis with the diversified Pilipino/Asian-American community in the S.F. Bay Area.

Pan-Asian Holiday Tour

I. South of Market -morning

Bessie Carmichael School health day fair
blood tests, urine samples,
medical display, demonstrations & exhibits
check-up check-out
rhythmic clapping of bamboo poles
brown bodies gettin' down to greez
on hot kanin, adobo & lumpia
a box of mcdonald's cookies for dessert
kali -stick-fighting manifestations
of a fiercely proud & transplanted culture
pinoy pilipino party -merienda in a makeshift
miniature manilatown -glistening in
the incandescent smile of a south of market
sun - while the headlines read of four young pinoys
arrested for robbery & 1st degree murder
-to be tried as adults
-presumed guilty until
proven innocent

II. J-Town -midday

Post-Oshogatsu luncheon
sharing sake', sushi, teriyaki chicken
-richard wada brings bottle after bottle
of hot sake' emptied into cross-cultured
bellies & minds of asian poets -
Al, George, Jayo, Lane & Doug
-sitting in circle getting drunk
toasting love & marriage and whatever else
is new or worth remembering in the languid
softening of afternoon sky -salmonstreaked
sun setting trembles the unsuspecting heart
-humbles the soul - to pause in the attitude
of worship as music of koto strings drifts
in with a soft breeze -filling the mind
soothing the spirit in J-Town
while a young nisei sister
alienated from her community
-from herself - o.d.'s on the poison of indifference
-on the heroin of futility

III. Chinatown/Dragon dies -evening

Dragon dances down Kearney Street
lights atop multi-colored 100 ft. long ancient emblem
symbolic of year's end - weaving now disappearing down
jackson street - snakedancin to drill teams
and floats with beauty queens & silver-dollar
civic-leaders & politicians
-snakedancin to the same ol' shit
-to a new succession in the measurement
of man's unforeseen & unknowing fate
firecrackers, cherrybombs, barrelbombs
EXPLODE as bodies push & jostle
each other for a better view
-getting away from the crowd
at the playground at commodore stockton
school -look out on a clear & cool evening
-the moon resplendent next to the transamerica pyramid
-while a loud-mouth blue-clad pig
in front of city hall yells
"hey ching chong!" to a middle-aged
chinese woman waiting for her ride

IV. Midnight

Sorcery of snakes has caught me
naive and unaware . . .
dragon disappears . . .
i hear the ripple of ocean
                            submergence
listen to a king cobra hissing
ready to strike
above my head

Still
i sing to the enduring enchantment
of eastern eyes
weeping in the wake of wasted lives
amidst the ignorance & dull oppression
                            of human joy &
                            sorrow . . .

The New Manong

At sunset -I have a vision of 10,000 carabaos,
dusky and caked with mud -like after a hard day in the
ricefields -10,000 carbaos slowly rambling down Kearney Street
heading toward broadway and the blazing blood-red sunset
And riding on top of the carabaos are the manongs-dressed in
their sabong-proud finest in 3-piece suits, meticulous in mackintosh,
spit-polished spats and fedoras 1940 style, brims tilted stylishly atop
balding, pomade-scented heads -I see manong after manong -Manong
    Claudio
Domingo, Manong Felix Ayson smiling in the sun, Manong Espiritu
    cackling
to invisible island spirits; Benny Gallo,Felix DelosReyes,Brother Willie
and Phillip VeraCruz riding slowly down the street -I see Wahat
    Tampao,
loin-cloth underneath tribal cloak, sucking on his pipe, looking like an
island nobleman/datu staring straight ahead -manong after manong
I even spy Manong Joaquin Legaszpi, a bemused expression on his
    creased
weather worn face -a cloud of smoke, dust from the carabaos' hooves
    mixed
with salem smoke, whirls about him like a halo, astride his mount ...
I am standing in front of the International Hotel, clean & sparkling,
the way it must have looked back in the early 1900's -just built
melancholy music playing from mandolins,12-string guitars, hawaiian
ukeleles coming from Tino's barbership -I look up and see
    Mrs. DelaCruz
gazing out the window -a pungent odor of sinigang & adobo
wafting down onto the streets -Mrs. DelaCruz telling everyone to
    eat-Kumain ka!
The carabao caravan continues down Kearney Street -endlessly ....
Manongs in suits and manongs wearing only loincloths & capes
    marked with
tribal colors & designs -carrying spears & shiney bolos -waving to all
the ladies -mink-lined perfumed blondies & shy young pinays lining
    the streets
The whole city is there -everyone crowding the streets -multi-colored
    children
sitting on the sidewalk curb -excited children laughing playing in
    portsmouth
square -playing everywhere -people looking on at the spectacle -sacred
    and
somber, religious in its conception -yet everyone seems in a festive
    mood ....
I hear tribal drums reverberating from the roof of the International
    Hotel
and the Bell Hotel; from atop the transamerica pyramid -echoing
    in the dusky
air -clanging onto the concrete canyons below -and mixed with
    the music

coming from Tino's as well as Mike's barbershop across the street
    I hear
the clean clear melodious sounds of noseflutes coming from distant
    hilltops
-rumbling like monsoon thunder -thousands of maya birds cover
    the sky and
fill the coral air with songs of long ago & faraway... I look
    around me thru
the mist & swirling haze and see familiar faces, new and young faces
    reflect-
ing the asian landscape in america -we are the new manong
The carabaos are bleating & bellowing -now disappearing long
    with the manongs
-past broadway and into
    burning   the
    bleeding
    sun

*Sabong - Fighting cock
 Kumain ka - "Come, eat!"
 sinigang - tangy soup-like broth with shrimp or fish
 maya - a common bird in the Phillipines, similar to sparrows

Arthur Sze

Arthur Sze was born in New York City in 1950, and attended the University of California at Berkeley. He has participated in the New Mexico Poetry-in-the-Schools project, done adobe construction work, and also conducted a writing workshop with women inmates at the Penitentiary of New Mexico. In 1982, he received a National Endowment for the Arts Fellowship. He currently lives in Santa Fe with his wife, Ramona Sakiestewa, and son, Micah.

His published books are: Dazzled, Floating Island Publications, 1982, Two Ravens, and The Willow Wind, Tooth of Time Books, 1976, 1981.

Moenkopi

Your father had gangrene and
had his right leg amputated, and now has diabetes
and lives in a house overlooking the
uranium mines.
The wife of the clown at Moenkopi
smashes in the windows of a car with an ax,
and threatens to shoot her husband
for running around with another woman.

A child with broken bones
is in the oxygen tent for the second time;
and the parents are concerned he
has not yet learned how to walk.
People mention these incidents
as if they were points on a chart depicting
uranium disintegration. It is all
accepted, all disclaimed.

We fly a kite over the electrical
lines as the street lights go on:
the night is silver, and the night
desert is a sea. We walk back
to find your grandfather working in the dark,
putting in a post to protect peaches,
watering tomatoes, corn, beans—making them grow
out of sand, barren sand.

Dazzled

Reality
is like a contemporary string
quartet:

the first violinist puts on a crow's head.
And the cellist

soliloquizes on a white lotus
in the rain.

The violist discusses
love, rage, and terror.

And the second violinist reports on the latest coup
in Afghanistan.

A gazelle leaps
in October light.

I am dazzled.

Black Lightning

A blind girl
stares at me,
then types out ten lines
in braille.

The air has a scent
of sandalwood and
arsenic; a night-blooming cereus
blooms on a dark path.

I look at the
short and long flow
of the lines:
and guess at garlic,
the sun, a silver desert rain,
and palms.

Or is it simply
about hands, a river of light,
the ear of a snail,
or rags?

And, stunned, I feel
the nerves of my hand flashing
in the dark, feel
the world as black
lightning.

The Cloud Chamber

A neighbor
rejects chemotherapy and the hospital;
and, instead, writes
a farewell letter to all her friends
before she dies.

I look at a wasp nest;
and, in the maze of hexagons,
find a few
white eggs, translucent, revealing formed wasps,
but wasps never to be born.

A pi meson in a cloud chamber
exists for a thousandth of a second,
but the circular track
it leaves on a film
is immortal.

The Chance

The blue-black mountains are etched
with ice. I drive south in fading light.
The lights of my car set out before
me, and disappear before my very eyes.
And as I approach thirty, the distances
are shorter than I guess? The mind
travels at the speed of light. But for
how many people are the passions
ironwood, ironwood that hardens and hardens?
Take the ex-musician, insurance salesman,
who sells himself a policy on his own life;
or the magician who has himself locked
in a chest and thrown into the sea,
only to discover he is caught in his own chains.
I want a passion that grows and grows.
To feel, think, act, and be defined
by your actions, thoughts, feelings.
As in the bones of a hand in an X-ray,
I want the clear white light to work
against the fuzzy blurred edges of the darkness:
even if the darkness precedes and follows
us, we have a chance, briefly, to shine.

Magnetized

Jimson weed
has nothing to do
with the blueprint of a house,
or a white macaw.

But an iron bar,
magnetized, has a north and south
pole that attract.
Demagnetized, it has nothing
at either end.

The mind magnetizes
everything it touches.
A knife in a dog
has nothing to do
with the carburetor of an engine:

to all appearances,
to all appearances.

Photo by Harry Fong

Jeff Tagami

I was born July 4, 1954 in Watsonville, California. I am Filipino American. My father emigrated to this country in 1930. My mother was born in Hawaii in 1922 and was raised around Monterey's Cannery Row where my grandparents cleaned squid.

I grew up on isolated farmhouses along the Pajaro River and Freedom, California. All my brothers and sisters and I learned hard work at an early age helping with the harvest of our parents who sharecropped strawberries, or, later manicuring the elaborate gardens of the landlord's ex-house in which we were allowed to live, rent-free, since my father was foreman of his artichoke ranch, and still is today. For recreation we built tree houses, floated up river to the Pacific on leaky rafts, or, simply, beat each other up.

Presently, I live, work, attend writing classes in San Francisco. My poems have appeared briefly (and disappeared just as briefly) in The Greenfield Review, Transfer, and a somewhat politically censored book in the Philippines.

Stonehouse

Here, in the hidden palm of the Pajaro Valley
A dirt road, overgrown with weeds and wild
Mustard where tires have not laid
Their tracks, disappears in a thicket
Of tangled bush berries.
At the nape of a mountain,
A stone house sinks into the earth
In a slow burial.
It is here, too, where we find
The aluminum ladder
Silver and dwarfed by immense apple
Trees drooping with swollen fruit.

We begin ceremoniously,
As if the trees were our grandmothers,
And solemnly undress them to bathe
In the warmth of their age,
Dark years old.
Death looms in the fog above
Our heads as we descend the ladder;
Each step measured, foreboding.
Our legs quiver from the bags
Strapped and brimming on our bellies.
Like unborn babies, they shift
Threatening our balance.
All day we work
Until dusk drives us from the orchard.

Afterwards, in the glowing light
Of the trailer
We sip beer and talk
Of the man in the stone house
Who, lonely for a wife,
Hanged himself in the warm lap
Of one tree—in the innermost
Secrecy of its gown of leaves.
The man who,
As our muddied fingers probe
Skyward for the last red bulb,
Gently shakes our ladder.

Without Names

In the yard choking
With weeds
Near the picket
Fence unpainted
Father slits the jugular
Of the goat drunk
On vinegar, hoofs
Wired together
Like a bundle of firewood.
The cry it makes
Is no louder than Elvis
Crooning off the needle,
Or the sigh sister gives
As she hugs herself,
Imagines her bed
Is a ship sailing
To Blue Hawaii.
She can't hear
My giggling on the porch
At the puppy lapping
My ear, or brother saying,
"Let it lick your dick."

Back of our farmhouse
Filipinos hunchbacked
From a lifetime of hauling
Irrigation pipes,
Squeeze goat entrails clean,
Sticking their fingers
In places I think
Not possible.
Around the fire
They squat and eat
With their fingers
The sweet meat
Dipped in blood,
Drink the green bile
For long life.

Night
And what it uncovers
Is this:
A smouldering pit
And the charred horns
Of a goat.
Sister rolling down
Her bobby socks.
Myself and my five
Brothers bunked
In one bedroom.
Father undoing
His trousers.
Mother slipping off
Her dress, hoping
For another girl.
The ripening strawberries
Surrounding us like an ocean,
To drown us in work
The next day.
And my father whispering
Above it all,
"It is so good, so good,
I forget my name."

Now It Is Broccoli

My mother who loses a piece
of herself each day
is bowing before the conveyor belt
as a river of broccoli
rolls by under the fluorescent.
All night
at the canneries of J.J. Crosetti
she trims the yellow and bunches the green.
Trims and bunches.
Until the colors blend
and she is lost
before this river of one color
that is neither green nor yellow
and unable to hold it back
lets it slip past her.
She remembers, once, in another shed
slicing off part of her index finger.
It wasn't the pain
or horror she remembered
but how the day was hot
and the shade of the corrugated
tin roof bore down cool
on the back of her neck
and the metal click
of the spinning rollers
echoed in her ears
long after the crates had passed.
It wasn't the kindness
of the floor lady turning off the machine
that she wanted to remember—
the floor lady who would just as soon
bark at her like a dog.
It wasn't the concern
of the forklift driver who searched
between the chopped heads of cabbage
thinking the finger could be sewn back.
No, it was the face
she longed for, that serene
face she lost years ago.
A face the young woman
across from her now owned
who did not once look up from her work
who smiled
as if remembering a silly joke
or the slight tremble
of her boyfriend's lips
as he kissed her goodnight.
Now she keeps the finger in the freezer
in an envelope with a plastic window.

Because it is still a part of her
she cannot let go, like her man
who pickled her miscarriage
in a bottle of alcohol could not let go.
For two years
he kept it beside the bed.
Each night he held it up to the lamp
stroking the glass clear of his choked breath
as if to contemplate a son without future.
Finally, as if that bottle
could no longer contain his grief
he buried it beneath the porch steps
near the mint.
Now it is broccoli
and my mother must be careful
though she has given up forty years
to the passing of vegetables
though she knows the knife
and the fat clumsy fingers
that betray each other
though she knows
broccoli is only a river
through which we carve our simple life.
Her raised knife wavers in the air
while the colors go on playing tricks
with her eyes, and the nail
of her clipped finger
slowly turns black
behind the box of frozen peas
and ice cubes.

The Foreman's Wife

I know the gun
its handle is made to fit my hand
its trigger quick

I know the dark chamber
and the six flathead bullets
we stay up nights to make

You show me the target
and I puncture the center circle
like the butcher's blade to my womb

Here is our trailer
my one checkered dress, my pants
my boots, my picking sack

Here are my darling baby
Chihuahuas yapping
and shivering in the cold

Outside it is pitch black
and the apples grow
fat as birds in the trees

In the next trailer three men
who are drunk play cards
Francisco, a frog voice says again

Ay, Francisco, there's trouble
and when you leave with your cocked
forty-five, I've reached for my thirty-eight

simply, like an apple from the branch
I am sitting on the bed
I imagine the playing cards falling

like leaves in the orchard
the headless bodies falling from chairs
and the long hooked-nose celery knife

By the time you slide
across the bloody floor
I can't make up my mind

whether to let you touch me
where the sun hasn't leathered my skin
or drill you full of holes

like worms through an apple

The Horn Blow

All day pounding nails
with an air hammer
the sound as loud as a gun,
I can hardly hear Franky singing
some nonsense lullaby.
Today, it's pig gates
and the boss wants 400
before the rains come down.
Forklift drops another unit
of wood, we pop in a cartridge
of two-inchers and start shooting.
When the oil smoke
clears, I see it is Franky who coughs
and coughs until his black
tongue hangs out and sawdust
settles like snow
on his mustache.
Beyond our table
the sawmen are busy
watching out for what fingers
they have left. Above their heads
they hang crosses, a rubber duck,
blond dolls.
If not for luck, then to pray
against a spastic knee
that brings the spinning blade
down like an axe
sending fingers or a whole hand
flying to heaven.
To daydream is to lose a part of you.
Ask Blanquet's three severed
fingers, ask Franky, the crazy one,
who will hide his hand in his sleeve
and hold it before you to shake.
And it is his hands
cracked and raw
that never heal.
Shotgunned stomach. One-kidney-Franky.
One hot day he revealed
that stomach to me, slowly raising
his T-shirt, and proclaimed
it the Map of California.
I saw the deadened nerves,
I saw the network of blue veins
leading to nowhere,
or here, his ramshackle house
leaning on its bad foundation
behind this lumberyard of new wood.
I knew then

it was a map of all the places
he's never been,
and if there were names of cities,
he could neither read
nor write them.
I knew nothing could kill him,
not even himself.
Now he faces me across the work table
in his one gray jacket, grease
stained and too thin
to be of any use.
He is picking at a splinter
lodged deep in his palm
like a new vein
and throbbing.
He looks up at the clouds,
calls the rain
to come down, You, Mother.
But it doesn't.
We work until muscles grow
even in our fingers.
When the horn goes off
signalling the end of work,
it is Franky who turns
to me with the wisdom
of all his 29 years
and says, "The horn blow!"
So I follow him, stumbling
through the nail strewn path
with no questions asked
past the stacked bins and pallets
because the horn blow.
Out the gate
through the darkness
we head for home
before the flood lights
blink on and the saws grind
to a stop
baring their crooked grins.

Photo by Shinga Tomine

Ronald P. Tanaka

Ronald Phillip Tanaka was born in the Poston Relocation Center, Arizona in 1944. He is the son of William S. and Mariko Tanaka of Madera, California. He grew up in the central valley region of California before attending school at Pomona College and the University of California, Berkeley where he took his Ph.D. in British literature and literary theory in 1971. He taught literature and linguistics for three years at the University of British Columbia before coming to California State University, Sacramento where he is now Professor of Ethnic Studies and English. Tanaka's publications include a volume of poems, The Shino Suite, Systems Analysis for Literary Macro-theory *and* On the Metaphysical Foundations of a Sansei Poetics *(serialized in the* Journal of Ethnic Studies).*He holds a black belt in* kendō, *collects Japanese pottery and is an avid though inept cyclist. He currently resides in Sacramento with his wife, the former Jo Ann Masayo Oki, and has a daughter, Shinobu, from a previous marriage.*

Selections from *Ogesa Ondo,*
Opus 1, No. 1 (1969-1975)

the big *trimmer*

> *hatarakedo hatarakedo nao waga kurashi*
> *raku ni narazari jitto te o miru.*
> *—ishikawa takuboku*

i am your big *trimmer,*
eight years old.
i smell of dried grass and
gasoline, though
we both take a bath at least
once a day.
(it's like your fingers that
never get clean.)

yeah, me mada genki da yo,
full of muscle;
my briggs-and-stratton sputter
but it never stop.

yeah, i'm just big and simple,
inaka mono.
        no fancy paint job,
        no rotary blade,
        no electronic ignition.

oh, i got my fault. bermuda grass
is tough sometimes, and dichondra.

remember when my roller chain broke
and i chew up all those ayame?
yoku oboete'ru na!

yeah, we been through a lot,
so when it gets hot,
i want to work harder for you,
isshō kenmei gardener.

but i guess me getting old too.
my catcher will always be
mendokusai, and i never
turn those corner like a *lawnboy.*

(now i wake up saying,
"mata atsuku naru ka?")

oi! masa-kun! ikō!
let's start early!

take the handle
where my green paint
has worn away.

(but be careful
when you pull me
off the truck, o.k.?)

soon the morning sun will
break across the trees

and the wet grass will
cling to us,

as we move across the lawn together,
as you sing *kari boshia kiri uta,*

>   and i sneeze,
>   and you sneeze,
>   and i sneeze.

sacramento 1973

snacks

—for haruo tamano

as the fog lifts over
the river,

the boat sways in the
current

to the tapping of our
poles.

glad to get some sun,
we break out

the coffee and snacks.
i watch how

carefully he pours my
coffee

and finds the blueberry
roll

because he knows i like
blueberries.

i settle into the bow,
and press

the steaming cup against
my face,

praying that some lovely,
silver-sided

salmon

should take his shining
lure, and run,

dashing, toward the sea.

sacramento, 1975

Drawing by Karen Sjöholm

Kitty Tsui

Kitty Tsui is a feminist writer, artist and actor. She writes from her experiences and insights as an Asian woman living in Gold Mountain and believes that art, politics and life are inseperable. She was born in the City of Nine Dragons, Hong Kong, in the year of the Dragon.

it's in the name

i've been called   sway
                       sue
                       suey
                       suzy
                       tissue
                       ha-chiew.

my father pronounced it choy
so i grew up saying choy,
always careful to add: t-s-u-i.

the first name is kit fan,
fragrant purity.
but can also mean
marriage.
in chinese, choy
can also mean hurry, fast, *faidee*.

i am constantly
chased by the chant
hurry to get married . . .

if it's not bad enough
it's in the name,
it's also in the face.

one day a woman instructor
insisted i had been
one of her guest speakers
in a class.

she was so sure of herself
she had me convinced
it was during my alcohol days
when memory was gone.

genny lim was the speaker.

it happens all the time.
orientals so hard to tell apart.

the same day
a woman stopped
to wish me a good opening.

i was not in a play or an art show.

zand gee, nancy hom and stephanie lowe
had a three-woman show.

that's not all.
i've been called
willyce kim,
canyon sam,
louise low.

it happens all the time.

a newspaper woman thought
i was willyce kim for months.
willyce kim gets called susan kwong.
nellie wong is made nellie kim
or not mentioned by name at all.
merle woo is called merle wong
or smeared as yellow woman
in a gay male publication.

it happens all the time.
it's in the name.
it's in the face.

orientals so hard to tell apart.

our faces,
strong, brown,
different as
the bumps
on the skin of
bittermelon.
our tongues,
sharp and fragrant
as ginger,

telling our history,
our experiences
as asian american women,
workers and poets,
cutting the ropes
that bind us,
breaking from
the silence of centuries

to write
our dreams into action,
give voice to our visions
and tongues
to our foreparents,

those who entered
at chinese hospital
or the paper sons
who came by way of
angel island,
forced to take
false names.

the sewing shop worker
the secretary,
the doctor,
the *deem sum* girl,
the lesbian,
the bike messenger,
the typesetter,
the boxer,
the student.

each with a name.
each with a face,

blood, bone, breath.

deem sum: baked, steamed or fried pastries that are a popular
Chinese breakfast or lunch food.

chinatown talking story

the gold mountain men said
there were two pairs of eyes
so beautiful
they had the power
to strike you dead,
the eyes of
kwan ying lin
and mao dan so.

kwan ying lin, my grandmother,
and mao dan so
were stars of the
cantonese opera
and women
rare
in a bachelor society.

when my grandmother first came
to gold mountain in 1922
she was interned on angel island
for weeks, a young chinese girl,
prisoner in a strange land.

when mao dan so
first arrived
she came on an entertainer's visa
and made $10,000 a year.

it cost $1.25 to see a show,
a quarter after nine.
pork chop rice was 15¢.

when theater work was slow
or closed down
other work was found:
washing dishes,
waiting tables,
ironing shirts.

in china
families with sons
saved and borrowed
the $3,000
to buy a bright boy
promise in a new land.

in china
girls born into poverty
were killed or sold.
girls born into
prosperity
had their feet bound,
their marriages arranged.

on angel island
paper sons and blood sons
waited
to enter *gum san*
eating peanut butter on crackers
for lunch and
bean sprouts at night.

the china men who passed
the interrogations
were finally set free.
the ones who failed
were denied entry and deported
or died by their own hands.

in 1940, the year
angel island detention center
was closed
a job at macys
paid $27 a week.
only chinese girls
without accents please apply.

my grandfather had four wives
and pursued many women
during his life.
the Chinese press loved
to write of his affairs

my grandmother,
a woman with three daughters,
left her husband
to survive on her own.
she lived with another actress,
a companion and a friend.

the gold mountain men said
mao dan so was as graceful
as a peach blossom in wind.

she has worked since
she was eight.
she is seventy two.
she sits in her apartment
in new york chinatown
playing solitaire.
her hair is thin and white.
her eyes, sunken in hollows,
are fire bright when she speaks.

the gold mountain men said
when kwan ying lin
went on stage
even the electric fans stopped.

today
at the grave
of my grandmother
with fresh spring flowers,
iris, daffodil,

i felt her spirit in the wind.
i heard her voice saying:

born into the
skin of yellow women
we are born
into the armor of warriors.

gum san, Gold Mountain, the name the Chinese pioneers called America

George Uba

I was born in Chicago, Oct. 12, 1947, lived in the Chicago vicinity for my first six years, then spent a year and a half in Missouri. Most of my life, though, has been passed in southern California. Probably my most vivid memories are of growing up on Los Angeles' West Side in the late '50's and early '60's. Although I have three degrees in English—a B.A. from the University of Southern California, an M.A. from the University of Michigan, and a Ph.D. from the University of California, Los Angeles—I began writing poetry comparatively late (I've been writing about five years now). I have taught English, however, for eleven years at four different colleges: El Camino College; East Los Angeles College; the University of California, Los Angeles; and, currently, California State University, Northridge. I reside in the San Gabriel Valley with my wife and two children.

I have published poetry in Poetry/LA *and was also the winner of the 1980 Academy of American Poet's Prize while a graduate student at UCLA, where I also founded and directed the Modern Poetry Group. I have published literary criticism in the* Colby Library Quarterly *and a critical review in the* Journal of Ethnic Studies *(forthcoming, Sept., 1983), as well as delivered papers at professional meetings.*

Old Photo, 1942

My father, fresh out of dental school,
decked out in short sleeves
and baggy slacks, his hair
cropped too short near the ears,
stands close to my mother,
his arm secretly about her waist.
My mother in white blouse and skirt,
in white bobby socks, in loafers
pressed together in a regimental line,
looks like a pretty schoolgirl
politely waiting for a bus.
They have recently become engaged,
hence the liberty my father takes.

Back of them is a double row
of barracks silently fronting
a perfectly level, unpaved space.
I know what is behind each door:
an iron stove of the kind
they no longer make,
a card table and folding chairs,
an improvised bookshelf,
and an army-issue bed
topped by the same stuff
the curtains are made of.

This is no military base.
There are fiberboard walls
stapled at angles to form rooms;
in the rooms are lives named
Tanaka, Funakoshi, Uba,
and pictures of loved ones
not yet eligible for war.
From the window there is a glimpse
of a gun emplacement, of a gun
secretly raking my parents
from the deck of a watchtower,
while, off in the distance,
over my mother's shoulder,
rises a solitary peak, Heart Mountain,
that my father could easily
cup in one hand.

All of this covers less
than half the photograph.
The rest is sky, Wyoming sky,
that, because of a trick of light,
appears the exact color of earth.

Gary Gotow

(Los Angeles, 1961)

Past the old barbershop on Jefferson,
On the stretch of road once halved by streetcars,
A block or so from the Enbun Market
With its specials hawked on fresh butcher paper,
And the Westside Okazu with its six red booths,
Steaming bowls of udon, plump chicken breasts,
And strips of beef behind a plate of smoked glass,
And opposite the retirement home
Set well back from the street,
As if obāsan with her perpetual
Broom had neatly swept it there,
Came Gary Gotow,
                Doing his loose-jointed
Shoulder-bobbing, burlesque strut
Like a bantamweight thug
Who'd copped the key to the city.
His right fist was curled like a creature of habit
Or the shape of tomorrow's bad news,
While his left hitched his pants
Impossibly to his chest.
And somewhere short of the 6th Ave. Playground,
Where battalions of Negro kids were choosing sides,
I caught a glimpse of Gary's gold tooth,
As he half-returned my hello.
I knew on one hip was a long-handled comb
To keep his ducktail slicked back, *evil*,
And on the other a razor
That would gladly have slit
Nostalgia's throat from ear to ear.

How Do You Spell 'Missile'?:
Preliminary Instructions in the Nuclear Age

Today we will speak in megatons.
Say salvo, ballistics, and payload.
How much makes a capacity?
How far a neutral zone?
Use target as a verb.

Today we will color in pencil.
Lead for all the cities,
Lead for the flowers, the trees,
And the name, newly learned,
Scrawled in the corner unsteadily.

Today we will count backwards:
Five   Four   Three   Two   One
Last is the thumb.

Firefly

(for my father)

A brown field jabbed a finger into a grove of cottonwoods.
That way was east and the splashy lights of St. Louis.
But night had fallen, it was time to turn back.

Far off I saw a figure moving with a rapid gait.
It was a man clad in a brown military uniform,
Advancing along the trail I had pretended to blaze.

As he worked his way up a rise, his heavy boots
Stamped the ground as if ridding it of spirits.

Then, as the stranger drew near, almost within hailing range,
I slid down a shallow clay bank and hid myself
Where ironweed javelined the damp bed of a creek.

And a firefly rose up out of the darkness.
I saw a large, hesitant hand reach out, too late! grab air.
Lonely its assault was. Then I rose out of hiding.

He said he was looking for his son. Had I seen him?

Then turned away, the back of his brown military uniform
Impenetrable and severe, like some habit resumed
Or envelope stiff with orders for the AWOL.

That was long ago. Nothing remains of that encounter,
Not the man or his gesture, nor the mission he was on.

And I have a son of my own,
Command his name, the hours of his waking and sleeping,
Patrol his movements with that keen-eared dog, Authority,

And am stunned by the thought of what small bright thing
He may someday recall and I may not—

Some speck of fire the night eclipsed.

Nellie Wong

Nellie Wong is a poet/writer/socialist feminist activist long steaming down the Chinatown U.S.A. trail, typing, filing and editing as a secretary in Oakland, California, where she was born in the Year of the Dog.

Active in the Freedom Socialist Party and Radical Women, socialist feminist organizations who work in the liberation movements around the rights of the most oppressed: women of color, lesbians, and women workers. She was first Organizer for the Women Writers Union.

Author of Dreams in Harrison Railroad Park, *a collection of poems published by Kelsey St. Press. Member of Unbound Feet Three with Kitty Tsui and Merle Woo, Asian American writers and performers.*

Co-featured in the documentary film by Allie Light and Irving Saraf, "Mitsuye & Nellie, Asian American Poets."

Wong's work has appeared in many journals, newspapers and magazines including Conditions, Poetry from Violence, This Bridge Called My Back: Writings by Radical Women of Color, Echoes from Gold Mountain, Bridge, An Asian American Perspective, Hanging Loose, Plexus, *among others.*

274

Funeral Song for Mamie Eisenhower

Excuse me if I don't weep
over your death, Mamie Eisenhower.
I mean in your position
as 'first lady' of the land
you were content to remain a wife and mother.
I mean the radio waves shook up my morning coffee.
Ah, yes, dear Mamie, quoted and beloved, I'm sure,
for not raising the battle cry of women
anywhere.

Why, Mamie, with your bangs curled
above your eyes, did you really say
you never understood why and from what
women wanted to be liberated?

And, yes, my ears wiggled, my nose twitched.
The broadcaster said this comment
was not intended, oh gracious no,
to put Rosalynn or Eleanor or Ladybird down.

But in groping toward truth and human liberation
I must say that a 'first lady' of the land
earns her respect from humankind
if she doesn't seek solace and anonymity
behind closed white house doors
if she opens her eyes and reaches out
to women everywhere in factory lines and offices
and lettuce fields

And, oh, I mean no disrespect
to the dead, a 'first lady' or anyone
'cause though my mah mah and bah bah taught me right,
my tears brim over the Melmac of decorum.

Under Our Own Wings

For A Sister, Merle Woo

Do not despair, my sister, of a brother's process.
Laughter connects to self-examination.
Laughter can be an opium poppy spreading
its poison first among ourselves. Our selves,
our whole selves, fragments, chopped liver
in a goldfish bowl.
To remain private with change is to self-destruct.
To go public with change is to begin
to challenge the forces of white supremacy.
Yet, good fortune, the good fortune of battles is not
simply opening red envelopes containing coins or paper money.
To believe that change comes about is to keep working.
As someone said, dear sister, as someone said,
you are always working, working
hammering away at lies, myths, distortions,
water hyacinths clogging the canals of Asian America.
Yet we are not property
to be sold, disposed, auctioned off.
What is antique, what is held valuable
is not necessarily unbreakable. A sea of faces stare
at our invisibility, our supposed assimilation.
A man believes simply that to err is to be human
and we sit and stir among whites, yellows, a few friends.
Ears and tongues perceive
the images of history swallowed in antiseptic schoolrooms,
on the battles of Vietnam
in the bedrooms, porno movie theaters, magazines,
T.V. screens of America.
Any wonder, dear sister, any wonder
that sisters and brothers must exorcise through ritual, form,
poem, songs, stories, essays, plays
at their own pace
the malaise of white America.
To create our own histories, culture,
restore our bodies to red health
to battle with every warrior beneath our pores.
Though we try   because we must
Though we try   because we want
to control our own destinies we are mirrored
in the windows of clouds
in the shattered glass
of our race and our sex.
How can we separate our race from our sex, our sex from our race?
And we hear again and again we must struggle
against sexism at the exclusion of racism.
And we hear again and again we must struggle
against racism at the exclusion of sexism.
These tactics. These words I must use, this language,
this tiresome but necessary chant. We in the midst

of struggle would love to ski downhill and breathe
nothing but fresh air. And I must ask:
how can we stand in isolation, how can we blow away
the blasts of destruction bombarding us from every direction
because we are
women because we are
colored because we are
feared?

The sagas of long steam ladies
The sagas of long steam men,
the talkers, the orators, the dancers.
They are here before us. We are here among them
brimming with language, music, air.
We birth ourselves, our privacies exposed
proud, seemingly free and yet devils nag,
polk at our very bones
to steal the art that is our lives
the magic that is our source
the spring that is our imagination.
To truly create is to struggle.
To truly struggle is to create
our selves, our processes of living, learning
and unlearning the garbage of self-contempt, of self-defeat
heaped at our own doorsteps. Sometimes we see no farther
than our own skins. Sometimes we prick
ourselves, savor the cactus of our own pains.
No despair, no struggle, no joy is personal.
If you begin, I begin.
If you breathe, I breathe.
If you sing, I sing.
And our tales are endless. Our tales begin
as the heads of dragons soaring
from the depths of our bodies.
To imagine and not only dwell within that imagination.
To live in our own skin and not only peel our own layers.
To join hands does not mean we always touch.
In art we open ourselves.
In art we gift ourselves our human joys, our struggles.
Nothing falls into our laps, not flower petals in the spring,
not even these letters that type words, language, experience,
validation. The silences break. The silences swell.
The silences weep and the skies once mute about our lives
thunder at our insolence, our daring, our strong yellow legs.
Let us thunder and become the wind.
Let our voices howl and let our voices sing.
Let Gold Mountain move and never stop.
In death our bodies regress to the innocence of bones.
In love we work to live in America under our own wings.

Song of Farewell

Why are you leaving
after all these many years?
Whose feet will I wash now?
Whose toenails will I trim?

Without you to share my soup
how many pigs' feet do I buy?
Will I smell the aroma of star anise
and will those cow brains
really make me smart?

Will someone serve you
peony tea, lotus bean cake
to satisfy your sweet tooth
during the Festival of the Harvest Moon?

Who will make your bed each day?
Who will sing your favorite wedding song?
And who will accompany you to Gold Mountain
and watch you dance playful as a baby girl?

New Romance

Poems are my love, my romance now.
A child of the 1950s when Marilyn Monroe crooned
to the persuasions of Tony Curtis. Ah, sweet
those days crusted with sugarplums.

Anxiety caresses my soul, stalks upon the earth,
a bobolink learning to walk. Rice fields emerge
behind China sunsets, above California hills.

Gold can be found, yes, but not only in the dreams
of my ancestors. Gold, though precious, that
which I wear in the shape of a golden dragon,
offers nothing but symbols of power, the process
of birth.

Voices regurgitate in the fountain of age.
Youth, long gone, wanders in search of memories,
anxious to settle on the noses of old women.

Gathering rice, I bend down and touch the earth,
know it to be my friend. Yet I fly, a phoenix,
into the heart of a sunlit heaven, where my sisters
study, cook oxtail stew, and walk on picket lines.

Shawn Wong

Shawn Wong's first novel, HOMEBASE (Ishmael Reed Books, 1979), won both the Pacific Northwest Bookseller's Award and the Washington State Governor's Writers Day Award. A German edition of HOMEBASE, titled BAUM DES HIMMELS, was published in 1982. He is also the co-editor of AIIIEEEEE! AN ANTHOLOGY OF ASIAN AMERICAN WRITERS (Howard University Press, 1974 and Doubleday, 1975), YARD-BIRD READER Volume 3 (Yardbird Publishing Co., 1975), and the sequel to AIIIEEEEE!, THE BIG AIIIEEEEE! (Howard University Press, 1983). His second novel, WOODEN FISH SONGS (Beverly Jane Loo Books/ Hamlin Ltd.), will be published in 1983. He is also the recipient of a 1981 National Endowment for the Arts Creative Writing Fellowship Grant in fiction.

Shawn Wong was born in Oakland, California in 1949 and was raised in Berkeley, California. He is a graduate of San Francisco State University and the University of California at Berkeley. He now lives and works in Seattle, Washington.

An Island

My humid hand against your
breast wakes me from a dream about us
where we move under straw hats
like lightning under clouds.

Without blankets we are intertwined
in the heat
your skin, warmer than mine,
holds the air between us.

It feels uncomfortable at first waking
and I want to move
the cool air through
our separate legs and arms.

You push against me
closing the spaces around us
as if we have slept like this for years
as if there is no heat.

Then in this tropical moment
an aspiration to move like the rain
crowds around us.
I feel my breathing in your body.

A golden fish melts against us
is found breathing where my hand rests
is found beating where your heart is
and there is nothing closer than this sleep.

We should make love now
in the moments when the lightning
flashes a light
into the folds of the sheets.

Periods of Adjustment

The first words spoken
when we return home
are sometimes a shock
when we've been included
in another voice.

The first feeling
in a dark room
of skin we knew
by heart
shows scars where we left them.

We call these moments,
periods of adjustment,
and we pass through them.

I've asked you about your life
the way I left it
expecting you to remain the same
until I realize the adjustment you made
until I place my hand on your stomach
and we know these scars by heart.

Lapis

You pried the oval jade
out of its setting in the ring.
Your heart gave up that green
for a lapis.
We held the ring in our hands
with no stone in the setting
a cavity of rough gold.
The other hand held the unshaped lapis,
"What do you think?"

Blue,
I am edged by it and bordered by it.
A tongue somewhere against the skin
burns a setting there
a liquid hand under a button of a shirt.
You dress me
and cut the stone.
You shape the lapis
hard edged on four sides with gold.

Blue,
the color of ink in the hand
the color of lake water full of sky
mirrored there.
We are mirrored and framed too
by your hand with the lapis ring
now polished
and holds my arm against you
my shape standing behind you.

A tongue against the skin
burns a setting there
a liquid hand.

Photo by Nancy Reiko Kato

Merle Woo

Merele Woo is presently waging a Free Speech battle to gain back her job as lecturer in Asian American Studies, U.C. Berkeley. She was fired because of protesting with students the elimination of activist lecturers, staff and student-tutors, of student participation in decision-making, of the original goal of an autonomous Third World College. She was also terminated because of being proudly outspoken about who she is: an Asian American socialist feminist lesbian. She is a member of the Freedom Socialist Party and the performing/writing collective Unbound Feet Three with Kitty Tsui and Nellie Wong. "Free Speech is absolutely necessary. If we cannot speak out at work, either in criticism of management or in regard to who we are—with truth, dignity and pride—then we are as enslaved and isolated as our ancestors."

Poem for the Creative Writing Class, Spring 1982

The silence in the classroom
of people I've grown to respect —
seems like so much potential here:
men and women
brown black yellow jewish white
gay and straight.

Classrooms are ugly,
cages with beautiful birds in them.
scraped, peeling walls
empty bookcases
an empty blackboard —
no ideas here.

And one window.
One writer comes in
from sitting on the sill,
three stories up.
We all want to fly
and feel the sun on the backs of our wings —

Inhale the breath
pulling in the energy of
seventeen people around me,
and exhale
putting out my ideas, ideas, ideas.
We all want to fly out that window.
A breeze comes in once in a while,
we want to go out with it
to where the birds are.

To take flight
using the words
that give us wings.

What is language after all
but the touching and uplifting
one to the others:
scenes
poems
dreams
our own natural imagery:
coins
a train to El Salvador
sleeping, pregnant mothers

menacing garages/a fist pounding/voices yelling
a yogi
cops being the bowery boys
roller coasters
blood
a girl on a swing
roses
water, streams, rivers, oceans
rise. rise.

Who can keep us caged?

The Subversive
for Nellie Wong

She rides a broom and curses God —
She gets burned at the stake if
    she isn't run through with it;
Her name is spoken in whispers because
    she has killed her children rather than
    let them starve —

She has no grace and swaggers;
picks her teeth with a dirty fingernail.
She's pushy and loud —
a voice like shirt buttons on a washboard.
How we hate her style —

We forget that she's helping us
    get what we want!
We forget because we're so busy
    being embarrassed and downright ashamed —
because she criticizes and yells,
    pointing a red stubby finger —

How gross! Send her back!
Let's just send her back right where she came from!

Yellow Woman Speaks

Shadow become real; follower become leader;
    mouse turned sorcerer —

In a red sky, a darker beast lies waiting,
    her teeth, once hidden, now unsheathed swords.

Yellow woman, a revolutionary speaks:

"They have mutilated our genitals, but I will
    restore them;
I will render our shames and praise them,
Our beauties, our mothers:
Those young Chinese whores on display in barracoons;
the domestics in soiled aprons;
the miners, loggers, railroad workers
    holed up in Truckee in winters.
                I will create armies of their descendents.

And I will expose the lies and ridicule
the impotence of those who have called us
    chink
    yellow-livered
    slanted cunts
    exotic
in order to abuse and exploit us.
              And I will destroy them."

Abrasive teacher, incisive comedian,
Painted Lady, dark domestic —
Sweep minds' attics; burnish our senses;
keep house, make love, wreak vengeance.

Traise Yamamoto

    The idea of an Asian-American poetry anthology struck me for the simple fact that very few have been done; there are few models to go by. I'm not sure what an Asian-American poetic is or can be, but I'd like to present some ideas.

    I don't think an Asian-American must or should, by definition, address itself to specifically Asian-American historical happenings. That is, I do not feel that it is the responsibility of a Japanese-American poet to write about the concentration camp experience, or the responsibility of a Chinese-American poet to write about their grandparents' dreams of the "Golden Mountain". Rather, I think an Asian-American poet should be infused with that cultural sense. That cultural sense that each of us carrries need not be expressed in a poem about making tofu or living in Chinatown—although it can take that expression.

    What I mean by "infused with a cultural sense" is that there is a certain sense of self that is imparted to each of use by our cultural background. Being as we are affected, consciously or unconsciously, by our culture, a poet's mode and sense of expression will, necessarily, be different, in some ways at least, from a poet of a differing culture. I do not mean to say that a radical difference results but is manifested in a fine difference of sense. We can see something like this in the very different schools of cultural poetry; Japanese haiku, the Chinese quatrain poem, the Italian sonnet, the French Provencal poem. Some impulse, and I almost hesitate to say this, led the Japanese poets in one direction, the French poets in another. That which was experienced by those poets sought to express itself in a particular form.

The poet Audre Lorde has said that there is strength in our differences, and I think she's right. Ultimately, our cultural differences must take a secondary position to the differences of each particular individual within that culture. I don't want to see a homogenous Asian-American poetic. Rather, I want to see a rich and varied poetic that encompasses each poet's individual voice, affected as it is with an individual experience of culture.

Prelude

I. Grace comes only after the long study of choice: the Bunraku-za masters knew this. It is in the three-jointed hand, the head jerked in surprise or fury, in the hem of the cloth pulled like feet stepping from the knee. After ten years, and ten years again, it is the arm braced squarely against the hip of the Master Puppeteer that pulses and contracts behind the doll; deliberate, passive. They are masters, and mean to be, and in this there is something sinister: they mean not to be seen. Dressed in black kimono and veil, what is not to be seen is soon not seen.

No one thinks about this in their own body.

II. There are places in the body that refuse the casual, the deliberate; where it has no elegies. There are preludes, the portico of daily life, ways of seeing: the sharp birdsong like the whir of cicada, the imagined meadow that lies fallow and dead in July; the stories between a mother and son, daughter and son, the lines of language, one to the other. Preparing the canvas for paint, scattered grain by the silo, the common names of things; the merry-go-round horse moving between the thighs, the woodturner's block: the belief that the body can dispell longing.

None of this prepares you to watch your grandmother getting into bed, how to stand and notice nothing so much as her pelvis shifting its weight, the propped knees, her grunts—the noises of effort, the motions of love: and only the desire to sleep, find rest. None of this is the sadness of a woman in a bathrobe late at night, the arbitration of anger. None of this prepares you for what you will choose to tell: tell, and retell.

In The VanGogh Room

1.
Winter pulls the body inward.
Tradition calls strongly, as if
in the act of keeping the belly
warm and rolled tight,
the milk in the coffee, the third
key on the ring, the touch
and smell of a lover
could become the familiar things of a childhood.
Perhaps this is why Spring makes us sad—
we think it is a delicate, attentive sorrow
for the small buds of trees;
but this June I realized it is because
Spring does not allow an inner life.
We are pulled from the body,
begin to wonder if it is the promise
of shedding the weight of our own heat,
close, that leaves us without cause or notice.

2.
The dimensions of the room are simple,
immediate, retentive. In this frame,
the refuse of a day surrounds the paint
like chatter. In this frame,
the quality of air: crow's belly, wheat shaft;
in this frame.
                    In this frame,
piecing the mind together
is an act of hunger. We ask
for nothing more. We take
what we have, hold to it
with gratitude, or without it.

The woman to my left says only,
"He must have been insane."
There is no fear in her voice.
It is easy to refuse
what we think is not our own.

3.
The fine bones of my hand
have nothing to say about God.

Diving for Pearls

Here, by the shore, we go out each morning
with the seeds of our children wrapped
in the warm folds of the loincloth. The sun
is still dark; the water, we know
will snap us into our limbs, a last touch
before we leave the smell of sleep
behind us. Each morning you tie
my hair back, settle it
down the center of my spine. Your touch
is no less simple than mine—still
it is not my hand that arranges
the hair, it is yours.

A simple pearl is not hard to find. But
it is the absence of the perfect, the purity
of shape that pushes us to where the water shallows
and then deepens.
                You stay above the water, balancing
your weight, as you must, to keep astride the boat.
You are proud that you have never fallen in,
but stand, legs apart; pelvis, the center
around which you place all weight. Your pride
is of not giving in to what you fear;
and you are afraid, afraid to fall
where strength is not a question of weight.

I come up for air, but do not come to the boat until
I have done, until I am tired and numbed.
You take the bag, a shell, then toss it
up, comparing the weight of it
in your palm with the weight of nothing
in your palm. For now, it is enough
that you have; that you have taken, as I,
too, take. I am woman
who does not want children; and so,
this jumping off, this diving into
an element that is no more my own
than it is your own, is an act of resistance. It keeps
the small wire-net basket full—
as a blowfish is full when it is frightened, before
it collapses back into nothing. For now,
it is mine as far as I wish it to be mine,
the sea; its pearls, seeds, children.

Biting Through

Hair splayed on the pillow.   I think: a Kyoto comb's the thing.

This road, they say, wavers at the far north point.
Yesterday I watched the trees at my back window,
and thought about the will of the traveller—
the things he must carry, the edge that must be cast
to keep together a single body of separateness.

The body plows in darkness; billow and fold.
It is learning to live this life of ache and release,
learning where desire is kept, where the body
knows its boundaries as the body
in love knows its boundaries.

It is like looking at the postcard of the Augustinian cloisters at
    Toulouse.
The light weaves between the columns, diffuses to a texture nearly
    tactile.

This is the third noon song they sing at harvest:
What was cut yesterday withers.
But what's cut today, what's cut today
withers, but look at the leaves of what's been cut
today.

Running the comb through hair is useless, repetitive without end.
But it is an act full of rememberances, and this is its importance,
    repeated
morning after morning.

These days, when the singulars of the man hobbling down the street, the
church spires in the distance, memories of coffee and pears by the river, fail
to come into a single line of vision, it is not enough to remember, "Flowers
are the seeds of things". It fails, as we fail. Such a small thing, to want.
Such a range of possibility when someone says, *This is what I have*
wanted. That is the song.
That is the song of our poor lives together, of the passing solstice, of the
trees after the cold snap, bare in the yard.

Photo by Vincent Hughes Frye

Cyn. Zarco

Cyn. Zarco, a native of Manila, is a poet-journalist based in New York City.

lolo died yesterday.
    they called him bill
    short for villamor
    i called him lolo
    lolo doming
    grandfather
    even though he was my mother's uncle
    even though he wasn't my real
    grandfather
    i called him lolo
    star barber at the star barber shoppe
    on 6th & mission
    he talked about the navy
    the american navy
    he showed me the calligraphy
    on his silver lighter
    he showed me his diploma
    from cosmetology school
    lolo
    lolo doming
    hung out with the boys
    at the mabuhay gardens
    gambled in reno
    got drunk with the pinoys
    kumpadres mga kasamahan
    died dancing
    on treasure island

Saxophonetyx

I've heard all about musicians
they take love/don't give love
'cause they're savin it for the music
Got to be so one night I was watching him
take a solo and when he closed his eyes
everyone in the club closed their eyes

The first thing I saw was my shoes
float out of his horn
my favorite leopard-skin high-heel shoes
the left foot then the right one
followed by my black silk stockings
with the seam down the back
my best hat and all that
were floating in the air like half-notes
as if they belonged to nobody
least of all to me

I tried to close my eyes
but I couldn't
out flew my blue silk scarf
my alarm clock
my alligator suitcase
even the last month's phone bill

He kept on playing that horn
as if none of this even happened
and when I slowly closed my eyes
I saw his fingers wrap around my waist
my spine turn into saxophone keys
my mouth become his mouthpiece
and there was nothing left in the room
but mercy

Teaching Poetry

(for Mark Strand)

You walk into a room of voices.
You are wearing a pink sweater.

It is snowing and a woman walks across the lawn.
She is naked and she does not see you.

You want her but the voices keep you from jumping
   out the window.
They are reciting poetry.

The woman outside is headless.
She motions to you.

You pull your sweater off.
Another pink sweater appears.

You peel off the pink sweater.
There is always another pink sweater.

You unscrew your head.
You feel much better now.

What The Rooster Does Before Mounting

Gustavo said,
"Your poems are like samba,
some even tango on the page
as if part of some strange ritual —
what the rooster does before mounting."

Gustavo said,
"In Argentina, I was in love
with Che. Even my father,
the old prick, gave him money."

Then, said Gustavo,
"You did not choose me; I chose you,"
and made me sit down while he took over
my kitchen.

I sat in a yellow chair
and watched him chop vegetables —

carrots   bell pepper   onions